The Politics of Ethnolinguistic Mobilization in Europe

Language constitutes a very sensitive nexus between the concepts of territory and community. Though a fundamental issue in contemporary societies, it remains relatively unaddressed by political scientists. This book promotes a better understanding of the connection between the concepts of identity, territory and language in the context of an enlarged Europe. We propose a portrait of the actual place of regional languages in European politics. Ethnolinguistic mobilizations have occurred in very different contexts, and their interpretation needs to take into account varying configurations and conditions of success that we label as situational, institutional, and socio-political. The book combines empirical case studies drawn from Spain, the UK, Poland, France, Ireland and Canada with comparative, conceptual and theoretical insights into linguistic uniformity and diversity. The various chapters in the book go beyond description. The originality of the work is to bridge the institutionalization of language regimes, the sociological analysis of language rights movements, and the normative underpinnings that ought to underpin language claims.

This book was previously published as a special issue of *Regional and Federal Studies.*

Alistair Cole is Professor of European Politics at Cardiff University, UK.

Jean-Baptiste Paul Harguindéguy is Associate Professor at Universidad Pablo de Olavide, Seville, Spain.

The Politics of Ethnolinguistic Mobilization in Europe

Language Matters

Edited by

Alistair Cole and
Jean-Baptiste Paul Harguindéguy

Routledge
Taylor & Francis Group
LONDON AND NEW YORK

First published 2014
by Routledge

2 Park Square, Milton Park, Abingdon, Oxfordshire OX14 4RN
711 Third Avenue, New York, NY 10017

Routledge is an imprint of the Taylor & Francis Group, an informa business

First issued in paperback 2018

British Library Cataloguing in Publication Data
A catalogue record for this book is available from the British Library

ISBN13: 978-0-415-72340-4 (hbk)
ISBN13: 978-1-138-38316-6 (pbk)

Typeset in Times New Roman
by Taylor & Francis Books

Publisher's Note
The publisher accepts responsibility for any inconsistencies that may have arisen during the conversion of this book from journal articles to book chapters, namely the possible inclusion of journal terminology.

Contents

Citation Information vii

1. Ethnolinguistic Mobilizations in Europe. An Introduction
Jean-Baptiste Paul Harguindéguy & Alistair Cole 1

2. Blocked Articulation and Nationalist Hegemony in Catalonia
Thomas Jeffrey Miley 7

3. The Jacobin Republic and Language Rights. Ethnolinguistic Mobilizations in France
Alistair Cole & Jean-Baptiste Paul Harguindéguy 27

4. Ethnopolitical Mobilization without Groups: Nation-Building in Upper Silesia
Magdalena Dembinska 47

5. Doing As They Are Told? Subregional Language Policies in the Basque Country, Catalonia and Wales
Patrick Carlin 67

6. On the Right to Linguistic Survival
Huw Lewis 87

7. Perfidious Hope: The Legislative Turn in Official Minority Language Regimes
Colin Haslehurst Williams 101

Index 123

Citation Information

The chapters in this book were originally published in *Regional and Federal Studies*, volume 23, issue 1 (2013). When citing this material, please use the original page numbering for each article, as follows:

Chapter 1
Ethnolinguistic Mobilizations in Europe. An Introduction
Jean-Baptiste Paul Harguindéguy & Alistair Cole
Regional and Federal Studies, volume 23, issue 1 (2013) pp. 1-6

Chapter 2
Blocked Articulation and Nationalist Hegemony in Catalonia
Thomas Jeffrey Miley
Regional and Federal Studies, volume 23, issue 1 (2013) pp. 7-26

Chapter 3
The Jacobin Republic and Language Rights. Ethnolinguistic Mobilizations in France
Alistair Cole & Jean-Baptiste Paul Harguindéguy
Regional and Federal Studies, volume 23, issue 1 (2013) pp. 27-46

Chapter 4
Ethnopolitical Mobilization without Groups: Nation-Building in Upper Silesia
Magdalena Dembinska
Regional and Federal Studies, volume 23, issue 1 (2013) pp. 47-66

Chapter 5
Doing As They Are Told? Subregional Language Policies in the Basque Country, Catalonia and Wales
Patrick Carlin
Regional and Federal Studies, volume 23, issue 1 (2013) pp. 67-86

Chapter 6

On the Right to Linguistic Survival
Huw Lewis
Regional and Federal Studies, volume 23, issue 1 (2013) pp. 87-100

Chapter 7

Perfidious Hope: The Legislative Turn in Official Minority Language Regimes
Colin Haslehurst Williams
Regional and Federal Studies, volume 23, issue 1 (2013) pp. 101-122

Please direct any queries you may have about the citations to
clsuk.permissions@cengage.com

Ethnolinguistic Mobilizations in Europe. An Introduction

JEAN-BAPTISTE PAUL HARGUINDÉGUY* & ALISTAIR COLE**

*Public Law-Political Science, Universidad Pablo de Olavide, Seville, Spain, **Cardiff University, Cardiff, UK

Although language is a fundamental issue in contemporary societies, it remains relatively unaddressed by political scientists. The aim of this special issue—based on the workshop 'Ethnolinguistic Mobilizations and Regional Languages in Europe' organized under the auspices of the Joint Sessions of the European Consortium for Political Research held in Munster, Germany in 2010—is to explore and compare the different strategies used by linguistic movements to defend regional languages in Europe. The title 'Ethnolinguistic Mobilizations in Europe' refers to the broad array of movements (including social movements, pressure groups, formal parties and political institutions) which defend vernacular languages.

The terms used to refer to vernacular languages can vary from one study to another. Nevertheless, 'vernacular languages' and 'regional languages' seem the most neutral expressions as they do not impose a symbolical hierarchy between the language of the state and the other languages spoken within the national borders. The state language is usually a regional language that historically was able to impose itself on the other ones. However, the focus on regional language clearly excludes the other tongues spoken in Europe, such as those imported by migrants (Swahili, Chinese, Arabic) or those spoken by very specific communities (like Hebrew, for instance). By using the concept of 'ethnolinguistic', we aim to study the political uses of languages spoken in different regions of Europe. We use the term 'regional' as a generic one, to signify that our analysis refers to the sub-state level. In practice, the areas of influence of these languages rarely fit neatly into the administrative regional subdivisions of the European countries; indeed, these linguistic areas encompass different regions from different states at the same time (as in Catalonia or the Basque Country).

Language Politics and Ethnolinguistic Mobilization

Language currently constitutes a very sensitive nexus between the concepts of territory and community. Ethnolinguistic mobilizations have occurred in very different contexts, and their interpretation needs to take into account varying configurations and conditions of success. The process of nation-state building in Europe generally used language as an instrument of political domination. In other words, language was used by state governments to produce consistent polities based on linguistic homogenization. Indeed, 'modernist' authors (for example, Karl Deutsch, 1953) identified as inevitable the underlying trend towards cultural centralization. The starting point of analysis of most articles in this special issue is the historical observation that the process of linguistic monopolization partially failed. Empirical research in this special issue demonstrates both the emergence of a variety of ethnolinguistic social movements mobilizing in support of a new deal for regional languages and the taking into consideration of this issue by central governments (for example in the Basque Country, in Wales or in Flanders).

The first social mobilizations in favour of peripheral languages, which occurred in the nineteenth century, were associated with political reaction and with political movements favouring a return to a pre-modernist society. Social mobilizations connected with political reaction remain a powerful feature of contemporary European society, of course, as demonstrated by the case of the far-right in Flanders, and the language component provides one important dimension of this. Attempts by political movements to invoke an idealized past are reasonably widespread regardless of where nationalist parties position themselves on the left–right spectrum. In the 1960s, the concerns of reactionary nationalist movements were relayed by new social movements (notably in Spain, France, Ireland and Flanders) framing language rights in the broader discourse of territorial identity and equality. In time, these concerns became converted into important issues on the agenda of regionalist and nationalist political parties. Language politics thus cuts across traditional cleavages and positions between left and right. The position of lesser-used languages also varies in accordance with the regulatory and legal stances adopted by particular European states. One obvious contrast is between those situations where regional languages were regulated 50 years ago (Irish) and others which are still being standardized (Occitan). The overarching contextual situations within which movements operate provide broad environmental constraints and opportunities that need to be taken into account.

In part, as a consequence of the above, the degree of institutionalization of ethnolinguistic movements can fluctuate. Some languages are supported by newly created state governments and thereby cease to be regional languages (in ex-Yugoslavia, for instance), or they are backed by an ambitious language planning policy led by a formal regional government (for example the Flemish). On the opposite side of this continuum other movements are composed by a simple network of cultural associations (for instance Breton). Institutionally, the political opportunity structure of European states progressively opened through the general trend of politico-administrative devolution occurred during the 1980s in continental Europe and during the 1990s in central-eastern countries after the collapse of the Soviet Union. The process of European Union accession (achieved in 2004 for most of the central and east European states) and the need to respect the Copenhagen criteria provided an additional incentive for newly democratic states to undertake measures to respect linguistic pluralism. This tendency was strengthened by the multiple initiatives adopted by international and European institutions, such as the UNESCO Convention against Discrimination at

School (1980) or the Council of Europe's Charter for Regional and Minority Languages (1992).

The institutional environment has grown more permissive, though, as the articles by Cole and Harguindéguy and Dembinska illustrate, the strategies adopted by language movements are influenced by the national state context within which they operate. Even within a state, however, ethnolinguistic movements themselves do not always constitute homogeneous communities. The relations between ethnolinguistic mobilizations and nationalist political movements vary across the cases considered in this special issue and more generally. On occasion, the use of regional languages and dialects can be purely instrumental, as in the case of the Italian Northern dialects spoken in Veneto that are currently being revived by the nationalist-populist *Lega Nord* to provide support for its discourse in favour of secession from southern Italy. In turn, other languages—like Sicilian—remain relatively disconnected from nationalist political claims and are supported rather by the cultural nationalist sector. Even where language promotion is central to social movements, their objectives are not always the same. Some language movements aim to compete directly with the main language of the state in order to convert their own speech into a hegemonic state language (as the radical Catalan activists); some other ethnolinguistic movements (such as the Welsh movements) mainly aspire to impose their tongue in certain institutional niches (such as television, radio, journals, and public administration); still others engage in a desperate struggle for recognition.

Studying Language Politics

The study of language politics in Europe has generated some interesting analyses over the last 30 years. A rather random, multi-disciplinary literature has emerged at the confluence of several academic disciplines, such as sociology, political theory, area studies, socio-linguistics and political science. This literature can be divided into five main groups that are presented below. The articles in this special issue each engage with one or more of these perspectives and contribute towards developing a comparative framework of analysis.

First, the pioneer investigations led in the early 1980s by sociologists on regionalist social movements (Bourdieu and Boltanski, 1981: 2; Touraine *et al.*, 1981) demonstrated that languages can channel the social, economic and political frustrations of regions with respect to central state governments. As such, language *can* be converted into the symbol of the centre–periphery cleavage. There is a close link between these classic political sociologists and more contemporary authors adopting a regional studies' perspective who have stressed the link between identity, language policy and nationalism. These studies have focused their attention on the relationship between language mobilization and regionalist or nationalist claims (Tejerina, 1992; Thomas, 1997: 323; Judge, 2000: 44; Cole and Williams, 2004: 554; Harguindéguy and Ballester, 2007: 89). In one way or another, evidence is produced of the capacity of language to produce social movements in most articles in this special issue. Most articles focus on a common set of questions around the modes of formal and informal representation used by ethnolinguistic actors. On the other hand, there is no easy correlation between national minorities and language minorities, as illustrated powerfully in the article by Jeff Miley (University of Cambridge) titled 'Blocked Articulation and Nationalist Hegemony in Catalonia'. In this paper, the author challenges the dominant depiction that there is a general consensus throughout Catalan society in favour of a strong language policy. This study is based on the comparison of the will of Catalan political elites to deepen the current language policy for Catalan with the moderate backing brought by simple citizens to this policy. As such, this study demonstrates a profound gap between civil society and political society. In other words, Miley shows the articulation of citizen interests is blocked since the Catalan Parliament is constantly producing legislation that is not backed by the whole population. In these conditions, the 'Catalanization' of Catalonia seems to be led by élites who have some real concern with the well-being of Catalans as a group but who also have concerns for their own power versus Madrid.

Secondly, political scientists focusing on the process of state (and nation) building have produced interesting analyses on how state languages converted regional languages into lesser-used languages through market expansion, mass-media, military service and the civil service (Allardt, 1979: 44; Shabad and Gunther, 1982: 443; Hobsbawm, 1996: 85; Klatter-Folmer and Van Avermaet, 2001; Romaine, 2002: 194). Such centralizing forces in favour of a state-wide language eventually provoked a reaction against the dominant language. In their article entitled 'Jacobin Republic and Language Rights. Ethnolinguistic Mobilizations in France', Cole and Harguindéguy show that the French republican centralist model is not as simple as it seems at first glance since it has not prevented the emergence of ethnolinguistic mobilizations in places such as Brittany, Alsace and Corsica. But the most interesting point is such movements have attained different levels of institutionalization. Mobilizing different types of explanatory variable (namely centre–periphery relations, the existence of strong local advocacy coalitions and political opportunity structures), the authors demonstrate how the politicization of ethnolinguistic issues has followed three different institutional paths even in the restricted state setting of republican France. In her paper ('Silesian National Identity: Institutionalization without Groupness?'), Magdalena Dembinska (University of Montreal) focuses on the ethnopolitical movement of unrecognized Silesians in Poland and the process of Silesian nation-building. The objective of her article is two-fold: on the one hand it aims to explore the development and mobilization strategies of the Silesian movement in its quest for language recognition and the institutionalization of the Silesian national category. On the other hand, it aims to verify whether the growing numbers of the mobilized Silesians correspond to the formation of a mass national consciousness—that is a nation. Her conclusions cast some doubt on the prospects of building new imagined communities based on bounded forms of national identity within a cosmopolitan Europe with fluid boundaries.

Thirdly, sociolinguists focusing on language policy have provided rather different insights. They have established important typologies according to the level of territorial extension and the constraint exerted by such policy (Fishman, 1974; Laitin, 1988: 289; Schiffman, 1996; Williams, 2000; May, 2001; Davies and Elder, 2004; Wright, 2004). Various levels of public administration are concerned by governmental programmes specifically designed to promote regional languages. Is there any kind of convergence at the level of regional language policies at the European level? Some answers to this question are provided in the article entitled 'Doing as They are Told? Subregional Language Policies in the Basque Country, Catalonia and Wales'. Patrick Carlin (Cardiff University) compares data from six sub-regional authorities in the Basque Autonomous Community, the Catalan Autonomous Community and Wales. In this absorbing article, Carlin analyses the efforts by these governments to plan for and implement language planning and policies through three sets of structural factors: regional demolinguistics, constitutional, legislative and fiscal provisions, and the influence of the political and institutional regional system.

Fourthly, there are obvious parallels between the above body of work and the recent interest of lawyers in the implementation of language policy, especially in Canada and Great Britain where consistent language policies have been implemented since the 1980s (Brett, 1991: 347; Schneiderman, 1991; Réaume, 1994: 118; Larrivée, 2001). In his article 'Perfidious Hope: The Legislative Turn in Official Minority Language Regimes', Colin Williams (Cardiff University) concludes the special issue by showing that the 'legislative turn' adopted by sub-regional authorities to protect and promote lesser-used languages is much more complex than it seems at first stance. The detailed analysis of the implementation of constraining language policies in the Basque Country and Ireland demonstrates unintended consequences in terms of professionalization, the legal relationships between the minority and the majority and between the individual citizen, the language community and the state.

Fifthly, there is, in turn, an obvious link between the frame of policy implementation and that of the underlying philosophical justification for a constraining language policy. Political theorists working on theories of justice have argued strongly that languages are not merely instruments used to lower the transaction costs of social interactions, but that they can also be desired for their intrinsic value. As a consequence, Western states have established three types of relations with minority languages: a neutral relationship with respect to all languages as asserted by liberal theory coming from the United States; the active promotion of all threatened languages, a claim forwarded by communitarians in Canada, Spain and Belgium; or a justification for the active support of just one language (or a group of few languages) based on a republican perspective thought to facilitate the political participation of all citizens (France) (Taylor, 1985; May, 2001; Kymlicka and Patten, 2003; Patten, 2009: 102). The following article is that of Huw Lewis (Aberystwyth University). In his article 'On the Right to Linguistic Survival', Huw Lewis endeavours to understand the ethical roots of ethnolinguistic claims. The Lewis study is crucial since regional language policies can exert constraints on the inhabitants of a territory (through quotas of regional language speakers among civil servants, for example, or the obligation to speak a regional language in mass media). Certain measures adopted to support language diffusion might transgress normative principles, such as individual freedom and equal opportunity. Lewis explores this question by focusing on one controversial aspect of language policy: can the members of a community, as individuals or as a collective, demand that they have a right to see the language survive?

This diversity of situations makes Europe a very interesting field for researchers on language politics. The aim of this special issue is to obtain a better understanding of the connection between the concepts of identity, territory and language in the context of an enlarged Europe. As editors of this special issue, we recommend these original articles to you.

References

Allardt, E. (1979), Implications of the Ethnic Revival in Modern, Industrialized Society. A Comparative Study of the Linguistic Minorities in Western Europe, *Comentationes Scientarum Socialum*, No.12, pp.44–63.

Bourdieu, P. and Boltanski, L. (1981), Le fétichisme de la langue, *Actes de la Recherche en Sciences Sociales*, Vol.3, pp.2–17.

Brett, N. (1991), Language Laws and Collective Rights, *Canadian Journal of Law and Jurisprudence*, Vol.4, No.2, pp.347–360.

Cole, A. and Williams, C. (2004), Institutions, Identities and Lesser-used Languages in Wales and Brittany, *Regional and Federal Studies*, Vol.14, No.1, pp.554–579.

Davies, A. and Elder, C. (eds) (2004), *The Handbook of Applied Linguistics*. Oxford: Blackwell.

Deutsh, K. (1953), *Communication: An Inquiry into the Foundations of Nationality*. Cambridge: MIT Press.

Fishman, J. (ed.). (1974), *Advances in Language Planning*. The Hague: Mouton.

Harguindéguy, J.-B. and Ballester, M. (2007), Acción colectiva y enseñanza de las lenguas regionales en Francia (1951-2006). Una primera aproximación, *Revista Española de Ciencia Política*, No.16, pp.89–108.

Hobsbawm, E. (1996), Are all Tongues Equal? Language, Culture and National Identity, in P. Barker (ed.), *Living as Equals*. Oxford: Oxford University Press.

Judge, A. (2000), France: One State, One Nation, One Language, in S. Barbour and S. Carmichael (eds), *Language and Nationalism in Europe*. Oxford: Oxford University Press.

Klatter-Folmer, J. and Van Avermaet, P. (eds) (2001), *Theories on Maintenance and Loss of Minority Languages*. Munster: Waxmann.

Kymlicka, W. and Patten, A. (eds) (2003), *Political Theory and Language Rights*. Oxford: Oxford University Press.

Laitin, D. (1988), Language Games, *Comparative Politics*, Vol.20, No.3, pp.289–302.

Larrivée, P. (ed.). (2001), *Linguistic Conflict and Language Laws: Understanding the Quebec Case*. London: Palgrave Macmillan.

May, S. (2001), *Language and Minority Rights: Ethnicity, Nationalism and the Politics of Language*. London: Longman.

Patten, A. (2009), The Justification of Minority Language Rights, *The Journal of Political Philosophy*, Vol.17, No.1, pp.102–128.

Réaume, D. (1994), The Group Right to Linguistic Security: Whose Right, What Duties?, in J. Backer (ed.), *Group Rights*. Toronto: University of Toronto Press.

Romaine, S. (2002), The Impact of Language Policy on Endangered Language, *International Journal on Multicultural Societies*, Vol.4, No.2, pp.194–212.

Schiffman, H. (1996), *Linguistic Culture and Language Policy*. London: Routledge.

Schneiderman, D. (ed.). (1991), *Language and the State: The Law and Politics of Identity*. Cowansville: Éditions Yvon Blais.

Shabad, G. and Gunther, R. (1982), Language, Nationalism and Political Conflict in Spain, *Comparative Politics*, Vol.14, No.4, pp.443–477.

Taylor, C. (1985), *Human Agency and Language*. Cambridge: Cambridge University Press.

Tejerina, B. (1992), *Nacionalismo y Lengua: Los Procesos de Cambio Lingüística en el País Vasco*. Madrid: Centro de Investigaciones Sociológicas.

Thomas, A. (1997), Language Policy and Language in Wales: a Comparative Analysis, *Nations and Nationalism*, Vol.3, No.3, pp.323–344.

Touraine, A., Dubet, F., Hegedus, Z. and Wieviorka, M. (1981), *Le pays contre l'Etat, luttes occitanes*. Paris: Seuil.

Williams, C. H. (ed.). (2000), *Language Revitalization*. Cardiff: University of Wales Press.

Wright, S. (2004), *Language Policy and Language Planning: From Nationalism to Globalisation*. Basingstoke: Palgrave.

Blocked Articulation and Nationalist Hegemony in Catalonia

THOMAS JEFFREY MILEY

Department of Sociology, Cambridge University, Cambridge, UK

ABSTRACT This article focuses on the representation of preferences with regards to language policy in Catalonia. By comparing social surveys produced by a variety of organizations with its own data, this paper demonstrates that there is a substantial gap between the political preferences of significant segments of the general population of Catalonia and the political preferences of their representatives at the Parliament of Catalonia. In particular, the language policy implemented by the Catalan elites is not consistent with the preferences of Castilian-speaking working-class citizens. The article identifies two mechanisms of 'blocked articulation' which serve to impede the representation of the preferences of these voters in the region's representative institutions. These mechanisms are: (1) the under-representation of Castilian-speakers in the region's representative institutions; and (2) the partial assimilation of elected Castilian-speakers into the attitudes and preferences of the Catalan-speaking, hegemonic fraction of the political establishment.

Introduction

This article will describe the dynamics of nationalist mobilization in one critical case—that of Catalonia in Spain. More specifically, it will focus on the limits to the hegemonic ambitions of the nationalist movement in the region. These limits are operationalized both in terms of demographic features of the Catalan landscape that fail to conform to dominant nationalist cultural and linguistic imaginaries, and in terms of lagging levels of popular support for nation-building policies (Deutsch and Foltz, 1963; Linz, 1993) that have been pursued by successive Catalan governments since the transition to democracy and rebirth of regional autonomy, with a special focus on Catalan language policy.

In Spain, there is an abundant normative literature centred on matters of institutional design for accommodating 'multinational' differences (Aja, 1999; Caminal, 2002; Requejo, 2005). A striking feature of these debates about 'multinational federal' institutional design is that they focus almost exclusively on the macro-level: that is, they focus almost exclusively on how best to accommodate, protect and guarantee 'national' differences between Catalonia, the Basque Country, and Galicia, on the one hand, and the rest of the country, on the other. Curiously, in these debates very little attention has been paid to the question of whether and how cultural, linguistic, and 'national' differences should best be accommodated, protected and/or guaranteed within these 'nationalizing' regions themselves.

As a consequence of the asymmetrical focus of normative concern and of related proposals for institutional redesign in the scholarly literature, the social scientific community has participated in the deconstruction of reified and monolithic Spanish-nationalist depictions of Spain; while at the same time, it has participated in the "reification" (Bourdieu, 1991; Brubaker, 1996) of monolithic regional-nationalist depictions of Catalonia (and, to a lesser extent, the Basque Country and even Galicia). This is equally true of the political-sociological literature on nationalism as a social movement in contemporary Catalonia (e.g. Castells 1997; Conversi 1997; Guibernau 1999).

This article will combat such reifications. It begins by highlighting a pronounced ethnolinguistic cleavage in Catalan society. It will then use this evidence to advance a revisionist interpretation of the dynamics of regional-nationalist mobilization—an interpretation which emphasizes the limits to the level of popular support for the regional-nationalist nation-building project underway in Catalonia—most notably, in the field of 'linguistic normalization' which has been pursued by successive Catalan governments since the transition.

The article will document disjunctures between the electoral constituencies of the main political parties in the region and their political representatives. Moreover, it will interpret these disjunctures as evidence of "blocked articulation" (Lindblom, 1990). The preferences expressed within the party system about nation-building policies do not register and thus block the articulation of the preferences of many members of Catalan society—in particular, those of working-class Castilian-speakers.

The article does not purport to provide a comprehensive account of all mechanisms by which such effective blocked articulation has been achieved and perpetuated. Instead, it offers a powerful—though parsimonious—account, at odds with dominant depictions of the dynamics of nation-building in the region, but much more compatible with the empirical evidence. Finally, the article ends with a discussion of more general implications of the findings presented here for both the theory of nationalism and empirical democratic theory.

Catalonia as a 'Divided Society'

Though it is rarely depicted as such, Catalonia can be accurately described as a 'divided society', in the sense that there is a pronounced 'ethnolinguistic' cleavage there, one which strongly overlaps with class and territorial cleavages, and which is reflected in patterns of neighbourhood segregation, partisan-political affiliation and policy preferences.

The terminology used to refer to different contending or potentially contending groups in a given society is always itself a matter of contention. The adjective 'ethnolinguistic' is employed here to describe the region's second most salient sociological cleavage—namely, that between (1) the group of people whose first language is Castilian, largely immigrants or children of immigrants from the south of Spain, who tend to identify themselves as Spanish nationals when forced to choose and (2) the group of people whose first language is Catalan (a romance language relatively close to Castilian), most frequently children of natives, who tend to identify themselves as Catalan nationals if forced to choose. The 'ethnolinguistic' landscape of the region is, of course, much more nuanced than this binary division suggests (Woolard, 1989; 1997; 2003; Boix Fuster, 1993), especially given the widespread diffusion of knowledge of both languages as well as patterns of multiple identification throughout the region (Linz, 1985). Even so, the term 'ethnolinguistic cleavage' nevertheless remains accurate in so far as it reflects the existence of two demographically substantial and intergenerationally consolidated and distinct, though inextricably intermingled, linguistic groups (Vila, 1993; Miley, 2006).

Throughout the nineteenth and much of the twentieth centuries, Barcelona was the unrivalled industrial capital of Spain. Historians of Catalan nationalism have frequently focused on factors directly related to the region's comparative 'overdevelopment' as crucial for understanding the origins of 'regionalist' consciousness and mobilization. In a particularly influential account, Viçens Vives (1961) emphasized the role played by frustrations of Catalan industrialists with the free-trade policies championed by a Spanish state effectively captured by a large landholding, southern agrarian elite in the congealing of regionalist consciousness.

More recently, Marfany (1995) has stressed the role played by xenophobic, anti-Spanish sentiment directed at the substantial numbers of internal migrants among the region's industrial working class who hailed from the underdeveloped south. According to Marfany, the birth of the nationalist movement at the end of the nineteenth century is inexplicable without reference to such xenophobic sentiments, which provided ideological cement capable of combining industrialist interests with popular support among the region's positionally advantaged, native middle-strata, in the pursuit of a 'Catalanizing' agenda. Though other historians have re-vindicated alternative, 'popular' roots to nationalist sentiment, most prominently traced to federalist versions of republicanism (e.g. Termes, 1999), in the wake of Marfany's *tour de force*, the challenges for those who would deny any causal links between industrial overdevelopment, a sense of quasi-racial regional superiority *vis-à-vis* 'African' Spain, xenophobic reaction to internal migration, and the birth of the regional-nationalist movement seem nearly insurmountable.

Over a century has transpired since the birth of the regional-nationalist movement, and much has undoubtedly changed in the interim—though much remains the same as well. The complex legacy of the Franco regime looms particularly large in nearly all accounts of the subsequent evolution of the Catalan regional-nationalist movement. On the one hand, the regime's roll-back of regional autonomy, its prohibitions on the use of the Catalan language in the educational system and public life, and other aspects of its aggressive propagation of a Spanish nation-building project all proved incapable of destroying regional-nationalist consciousness. In some senses these policies galvanized broad support for at least some of the aspirations of the nationalist movement across the spectrum of opposition not only in the region, but throughout the entire country, during the transition to democracy.

On the other hand, the regime's promotion of rapid capitalist development in the region, which experienced extremely high rates of growth between the mid-1950s and the general crisis of the 1970s, led to an unprecedentedly large new wave of internal migration to Catalonia. Indeed, the influx of former peasants largely from the south of Spain into the Catalan factories in the period, when they would come to constitute the core of the industrial working class in Catalonia, largely coincides with the re-emergence of regional-nationalist mobilization, which had been effectively beaten back into submission by Francoist repression for nearly a generation after the end of the bloody Civil War.

The temporal coincidence of the influx of mass migration and the re-emergence of regional-nationalist mobilization was not a coincidence, in a causal sense; it in fact contributed to the nationalist re-awakening, which awoke to express an imaginary reminiscent of so many xenophobic nightmares, rife with demographic anxieties expressed in terms of the imminent danger of the drowning of one's culture amidst a sea of aliens (Shafir, 1995). Indeed, at the time, Catalan nationalist intellectual circles were not immune from overtly xenophobic, exclusionary appeals to save the Catalan culture by constructing a demographic dam to contain the flood (Colomer, 1986).

National Language Planning Policy in Catalonia

It was against this backdrop that the regional-nationalist then-dissident Jordi Pujol would famously and 'generously' extend the discursive boundaries of Catalan identity to include all who "live and work in Catalonia". The influx of immigrants could not and should not be stopped. The march of capitalist development must continue. Given these circumstances, the only practical task at hand for true Catalan patriots was to get to work at "integrating" and/or "assimilating" the "new Catalans" (Colomer, 1986). By the time of the transition to democracy this 'integrationist/assimilationist' formula had become dominant within the regional-nationalist movement, at least at the level of its official discursive repertoire, though primordialist distinctions between '*xarnegos*' (people born in Catalonia with non-Catalan parents) and '*catalans de la ceba*' (people born in Catalonia with Catalan parents) were hardly erased, and indeed remained quite current at the level of popular visions and divisions of the social world (Barrera González, 1985; Delgado Ruíz, 1998).

The transition to democracy coincided with a reversal of fortunes on the economic front, as the Spanish economy proved incapable of escaping the general economic malaise of the 1970s. This economic downturn would profoundly and directly condition regional-nationalist dynamics in Catalonia in at least two ways: first, by abruptly ending the wave of immigration to the region; and, second, by simultaneously rendering employment opportunities increasingly difficult to come by. The Catalan economy would eventually pick up again, though employment opportunities would remain quite scarce, as the region would consistently register official unemployment levels around 20% throughout the 1980s and much of the 1990s (and again since the onset of the most recent crisis). Concomitant with this eventual pick-up, there would be an extension of social rights and basic services provided in exchange for the 'rationalization' and 'modernization' of the Spanish economy by the nominally socialist governments of Felipe González that ruled the country from the early 1980s through the mid-1990s, as well as an influx of European cohesion funds that did much to facilitate the growth of the south of Spain. Together, these developments meant that neither the 'pull' nor the 'push' mechanisms that had underlay the previous internal-migratory wave to the region would be triggered anew.

Nevertheless, the demographic 'damage' had been done. In 1982, shortly after the transition to democracy, fully 35.9% of the Catalan population had been born outside of the region (Linz, 1985). Two decades later, the proportion remained 30.8% (Orizo and Roque, 2001). The internal migrant population has thus posed a serious demographic challenge to the spread of regional-nationalist aspirations. This demographic challenge appears even starker when dividing the population according to so-called 'mother-tongue'—in 2003, only 43.1% of the population were native Catalan-speakers, compared with fully 56.3% who were native Castilian-speakers. In fact, by 2008, as a result of a new wave of migration to the region, this time from outside of Spain (largely Latin America and North Africa), the percentage of native Catalan-speakers had fallen further still, to constitute a mere 35.4% of the population in Catalonia (Direcció General de Política Lingüística, 2008).

Given these numbers, it is not a surprise that the regional-nationalist movement has consistently depicted the phenomenon of migration as a problem, even as a threat to the collective survival of the Catalan language and Catalan people (Pujol, 1976). This framing of migration as a collective-existential threat is crucial for understanding the dynamics of nation-building in the region. Indeed, the policies of 'linguistic normalization' and of 'national reconstruction' that have been pursued since the transition have had as one of their principal objectives the integration and/or assimilation of internal (and more recently international) immigrants and of their descendants into the linguistic and cultural habits of the native, Catalan-speaking population.

In the years following the consolidation of the Catalan regional government and its newfound control of the educational system and over linguistic policies, the governing conservative nationalist coalition *Convergència i Unió*, led by Jordi Pujol, would prioritize the exercise of this autonomy in pursuit of integrationist nation-building policies. These policies have been principally centred around the compulsory educational system and in the public sector, but also in the regulation and provision of large subsidies for the mass media under regional control. Successive regional governments have consistently consolidated ever-more expansive policies of 'Catalanization', with broad though not unanimous support among the main parties in the region, the consensus in favour of them including not only explicitly regional-nationalist formations but also crucially the Catalan branch (PSC) of the PSOE.[1]

At the core of Catalan nation-building policies is the 1983 *Llei de Normalització Lingüística* (LML) which was passed unanimously by the autonomous Catalan parliament. The 1998 expansion of it, the *Llei de Política Lingüística* (LPL), was defended not only by the PSC, but by the ex-communists of IC as well. Only the Spanish-conservative PP and sovereignist ERC voted against it. They did so for diametrically opposed reasons: the former objected to what it saw as the law's excesses, the latter to what it saw as the law's timidity. Nevertheless, together, the parties that passed the 1998 LPL—the conservative Catalan nationalist coalition CiU, the PSC and IC—received 78.1% of the vote in the regional elections held in October 1999. If ERC is included in the pro-linguistic normalization and 'national reconstruction' camp, only 9.5% of the vote went to a party, the PP, that stood in opposition to these policies (Miley, 2006; Levin, 2010).

A Consensual Language Policy?

As the main parliamentary representative of the Castilian-speaking working class in Catalonia, the PSC-PSOE has played a key role in silencing opposition to the project of 'linguistic normalization'—i.e. in keeping potential opposition to the project amongst its Castilian-speaking working-class base for the most part latent and, where salient, at least ensuring that such opposition remains marginalized and stigmatized with the status of an extremist ideology, condemned to the realm outside of reasonable and moderate public opinion. Had the PSC-PSOE taken a different stance during this period, had it chosen to oppose the regional-nationalist nation-building agenda, that agenda could not have advanced nearly as far as it has. In other words, the PSC-PSOE has played a critical role in helping the regional-nationalist movement achieve the degree of hegemony it has; for it has allowed the movement to silence opposition related to the 'demographic problem'.

The question thus presents itself: why has the PSC-PSOE taken such a stance? Party leaders and some social-scientists (Laitin, 1987), have suggested that this strategy in fact reflects the objective interests—or even actual preferences—of the party's Castilian-speaking working-class core constituency. They emphasize the potential benefits of linguistic 'integration' for immigrants, and especially for their children, in terms both of job-market opportunities and prospects for social mobility. In so doing, these party leaders have helped to assuage the demographic 'problem', so to speak, by re-framing the nation-building policies as policies that promote equal opportunity for all citizens in Catalonia.

The significant overlap between ethnolinguistic and class cleavages in Catalan society does provide certain structural incentives for the Castilian-speaking workers, and especially their descendants, to want to pragmatically acquiesce, actively adapt or even outright assimilate into the linguistic and cultural repertoire of the region's native middle strata, no doubt (Woolard, 2003). Even so, such upwardly-mobile individuals are exceptions who prove the rule. Though the vast majority of second-generation Catalans, unlike their internal migrant parents, can speak the Catalan language (due to their experiences in the educational system), they nevertheless tend to continue to use mostly or even exclusively the Castilian language in most spheres of their everyday lives (Secretaria de Política Lingüística, 2008). The same can be said for their patterns of national identification—in sharp contrast to their native Catalan-speaking counterparts—exceedingly few second-generation Catalans come to identify predominantly or exclusively with Catalonia, the vast majority continue to register balanced dual Spanish and Catalan identities (Martínez-Herrera, 2002; De la Calle and Miley, 2008).

If objective interests as reflected in the structure of underlying micro-level incentives for assimilation cannot explain the posture taken by the PSC-PSOE in support of the regional-nationalist nation-building policies, the subjective preferences of the party's Castilian-speaking working-class core constituency are even less satisfying in terms of their explanatory power. Survey data reveal that levels of support for the policies of linguistic normalization among Castilian-speakers has remained, at most, tepid. Indeed, a 1998 study commissioned by the Catalan regional government (in the year that the second language law was passed) determined that the overall population was almost evenly split over language policy in the region; and that among Castilian-speakers, fully 79.5% either openly criticize linguistic policy for being excessive or, at best, only passively accept it (Departament de Cultura, 1998).

The reasons many Castilian-speakers give for passively accepting linguistic policy have to do with the pursuit of social mobility in a context of regional-nationalist dominance. Catalan-speaking school is frequently presented as the unique way to learn Catalan well enough to pass the linguistic exams required for qualifying for good public sector jobs. This logic links the prospects of escaping poverty and achieving upward social mobility with exposure to immersion policies in the educational system. Note, however, that the link largely exists because of the parallel existence of a linguistic-policy regime that includes linguistic prerequisites for those aspiring to occupy good jobs, especially in the public sector (Solé and Alarcón, 2001). In other words, acceptance of nation-building policies in the schools is a rational response, given the existence of linguistic barriers to job opportunities, but these are themselves but the product of parallel nation-building policies in public sector labour markets. Mere recognition of hegemony can breed a certain level of acceptance, or pragmatic acquiescence to a given policy regime.

But the promise of social mobility for Castilian-speaking working-class people has amounted in large part, though not fully, to a hollow hope (Rodríguez Mora *et al.*, 2007). In fact, most good public sector jobs have gone to native Catalan-speakers (Matas Dalmases, 1995; Miley, 2006). Perhaps not surprisingly, the regional-nationalist nation-building policies have catered not only to the *preferences* of their core native Catalan-speaking constituency, but also to their objective labour market *interests*—with linguistic prerequisites undoubtedly contributing to the virtual monopolization by native Catalan-speakers of posts in the new regional administration, and to their capturing of the lion's share of posts in other public sector jobs as well, including in the educational system.

If neither the objective structural interests nor the subjective preferences of the PSC-PSOE's Castilian-speaking working-class core constituency can explain the party's consistent position in favour of regional-nationalist language policy, what can? It is argued in this study that the party's position, and by extension the political consensus in favour of regional-nationalist nation-building policies, is best understood as a product of effective 'blocked articulation'. In other words, the preferences expressed within the party system and government policies more generally fail to register and thereby effectively block the articulation of the preferences and interests of many members of society—particularly, working-class Castilian-speakers.

'Blocked Articulation' in Catalan Political Society

Before turning to elaborate two mechanisms by which this blockage has been achieved, a few words are in order about how to conceptualize the role of political parties and the nature of party systems in the liberal-democratic representative state; and about some basic features of the consolidated party system in the region. The political party, in the context of the competitive incentives built into multi-party electoral competition, constitutes one of the primary organizational means for channelling conflicts in representative democracies. Party systems involve, among other things, incentive structures that make parties compete against each other in part by, in principle, articulating the views of the mass of people that make up the basic units of modern states.

There is, to be sure, substantial reason, both theoretical and empirical, to think that parties do not merely mirror but also shape the opinions and views, perspectives and the like of the human beings that constitute the voting public (Przeworski and Sprague, 1986). Still, one aspiration of modern democratic ideology has been to construct party systems which articulate with a fair degree of accuracy pre-existing, exogenously determined public opinion. Indeed, this is why Robert Dahl (1971) goes so far as to conceptualize "polyarchy" (his neologism for representative democracy) in explicit contrast to 'hegemony', which he defines as a political system in which there is a low degree of articulation of divergent political opinions. However, there are a variety of ways in which the articulation and representation of many people's voices within the formal purview of democratic governance can nevertheless still be impeded or 'blocked' (Lindblom, 1990).

In the case at hand, the instance of blocked articulation has to do with the lack of opening of channels for working-class Castilian-speakers within Catalonia to express their voice in the region's self-governing political institutions, most emblematically, the Catalan Parliament. In other words, the 'supply-side' of policy options on offer among the main parties with representatives in the regional legislature is constrained. However, in order to verify the existence of blocked articulation and to ascertain the severity of the 'supply-side deficit', it is important to know a few basic things about the structure of competitive space for political parties operative in the Catalan electoral arena. It has frequently been noted throughout the post-transition period that "electoral alignments and interparty competition have been structured in Catalonia along two main attitudinal axes: the left–right axis, and the axis of nationalism" (Pallarés and Font, 1995; Pallarés 2000). These attitudinal axes are related to the two fundamental distinct but reinforcing cleavages in Catalan society: the cleavage among classes, and the cleavage between ethnolinguistic groups.

It is accurate to say that these two axes have structured party competition in terms of the social bases of support for the main parties and party coalitions that compete for representative posts. However, it is inaccurate to say that these two axes have structured party competition in terms of the policy options on offer—that is, on the political 'supply-side'. In general, political parties do not 'sell' just one policy associated with just one policy domain; rather, they offer 'bundles' or 'packages' of policies associated with multiple policy domains (Budge and McDonald, 2006). Thus, the 'supply-side deficit' to which we refer has to do with the 'policy packages' on offer in the 'electoral market'. In particular, the 'policy package' missing from the supply-side of policy alternatives on offer in the electoral market of Catalonia is one that combines a clear opposition to regional-nationalist nation-building policies, alongside a credible defence of redistributive, welfare-statist, or other social-democratic alternatives on the axis of class cleavage.

This is not to deny the existence of party competition along each of these axes independently. In fact, in relation to the region's pronounced ethnolinguistic cleavage, there are competitive parties that have offered clear opposition to regional-nationalist nation-building policies. Historically, the defence of such a policy option has remained largely limited to the Catalan branch of the Spanish-conservative PP. More recently in 2006, a single-issue anti-nationalist party, *Ciutadans* (Citizens), has even managed to overcome significant institutional and organizational barriers to entry and has obtained representation in the region's autonomous legislature—which is no small task in an electoral market dominated by consolidated parties and, therefore, a consolidated party system. Even so, no party has combined the defence of Castilian-speaking preferences and interests with a credible defence of redistributive, welfare-statist, or other social-democratic policies. This leaves working-class Castilian-speakers in the horns of a difficult dilemma: should they sacrifice their class-based preferences and interests by lending their support to right-wing or single-issue parties who appeal to their preferences and interests *qua* Castilian-speakers? Or should they sacrifice their preferences and interests *qua* Castilian-speakers by lending their support to left-wing parties who nevertheless appeal to their class-based preferences and interests?

This dilemma, a by-product of constraints on the supply-side of policy options, has not gone entirely unnoticed by scholars of electoral competition in Catalonia. Indeed, some scholars have argued that it helps explain low levels of working-class Castilian-speaking turnout, especially in regional elections (Riba, 2000), and a few have even spoken of "electoral market failure" (Lago *et al.*, 2007). Most analysts, however, have refrained from framing the results of the competitive electoral process in the region in such critical terms. Instead, the absence of left-wing opposition to regional-nationalist nation-building policies tends to be referred to in positive terms. According to this line of reasoning, support for regional-nationalist nation-building policies on the part of left-wing parties is best interpreted as a sign of political responsibility (cited in Miley, 2006). As such, leaders of these parties should be congratulated for having resisted the temptation of demagoguery in respect to Spanish-nationalist sensibilities among Castilian-speaking workers. Other analysts argue in the somewhat more normatively-restrained terms of rationality that the constraints on 'supply-side options' available in the Catalan electoral market are but the reflection of rational electoral considerations among left-wing party leaders committed to a strategy of catch-all competition (Pallarés and Font, 1995; Caminal, 1998). According to them, lack of opposition to regional-nationalist nation-building policies on the part of left-wing parties is best interpreted as an attempt to gain support among native, Catalan-speaking workers and lower-middle strata.

But such distortions in the principal–agent relation between voters and policy elites begin to make more sense when the resources at the disposal of the region's two linguistic groups are taken into account. Critics of liberal democracy have long complained that privileged groups have disproportionate *de facto* influence over the policy-making process despite formal equality of voice in the representative state (Miliband, 1989). This seems to be the case in the Catalan electoral market in which a positionally advantaged minority—in this case, the regional-nationalist movement, along with a core constituency of native Catalan-speaking middle strata—has managed to impose a particular agenda while portraying it as reflective of the 'general will of the nation'.

Mechanisms of Blockage

Let us now turn to examine a couple of specific mechanisms by which the preferences and interests of Castilian-speakers have been blocked from articulation in Catalan political society. To do so, 355 interviews were conducted with politicians and teachers between January 2000 and June 2001[2] and then compared with the rest of the population through a meta-analysis. This comparative method allows measuring with a relatively high degree of precision the similarities and differences between political elites and their constituencies in terms of policy preferences, identities, and demographic profiles. It also allows measuring ideological and network conflicts at different levels of hierarchy within and between political parties. For both of these reasons, elite–mass survey response comparisons provide a powerful methodological tool for detecting the existence and location of blocked articulation of the preferences and interests of party constituencies. To render the elite–mass comparison effective, we use surveys of the general public conducted as close as possible to the time that the elite surveys were conducted.[3]

The survey focused on attitudes towards Catalan linguistic policy in the educational system. Official policy in Catalonia has mandated that primary education be conducted basically exclusively in Catalan, ever since 1992, when the *Generalitat* decreed Catalan to be the language of instruction for all primary schools (Miley, 2006). The decree would later be ratified and extended to secondary schools in Article 21.1 of the 1998 LPL (Law of Linguistic Policy), and then included in 2006 in the new Statute of Autonomy as well. But this policy, so central to the nationalist agenda of 'linguistic normalization', cannot be accurately described as reflecting a Downsian median-voter style 'compromise' in the least. According to a survey conducted by the *Centro de Investigaciones Sociológicas* (Centre for Sociological Researches, CIS) in the same year that the LPL was passed by nearly four-fifths of the representatives in the Catalan Parliament, not only did this policy fly in the face of the 70.6% of Castilian-speakers who would prefer schooling to be conducted in, at the very most, equal doses of Catalan and Castilian (and arguably the 91.5% who would prefer for schooling to take place at most predominantly in Catalan); in fact, this policy even exceeded the preferences of at least 40.8% of the Catalan-speaking community (Table 1).

Comparison of the responses of the general public with those of political representatives at both the municipal and parliamentary levels (and with school teachers) confirms that language policy in the educational system, like language policy more generally in the region, is much more reflective of the attitudes and preferences of the politicians who make the laws and the teachers who implement them. It would appear that these political elites are actually representing themselves, more so than they are any particular constituency *per se*—though, of course, the attitudes of the Catalan-speaking community as a whole are much closer to official policy than are the attitudes of the Castilian-speaking community, whose preferences seem to be excluded altogether from the terms of 'consensus' reached by the democratically elected representatives in the region. In sum, working-class Castilian-speakers' preferences are being effectively blocked from articulation within the channels provided by political society.

Table 1. Preferred linguistic model for the educational system, by 'mother tongue' and ascendancy groups, elites versus masses (%)

		All Spanish	More Spanish	Equal	More Catalan	All Catalan	DK/DA	Total	*n*
Overall	General public	0.8	4.0	50.2	33.2	9.3	2.5	100	(1006)
	Teachers	0	0	22.3	36.1	41.0	0.6	100	(166)
	Local politicians	0	0.8	25.8	39.1	33.6	0.8	100.1	(128)
	Parliamentarians	0	0	23.2	25.0	48.2	3.6	100	(56)
Mother tongue	***Castilian***								
	General public	1.3	6.5	62.8	20.9	5.4	3.1	100	541
	Teachers	0	0	40.7	27.1	32.2	0	100	59
	Politicians	0	0	37.7	39.6	22.6	0	99.9	53
	Catalan								
	General public	0	0.8	32.8	49.9	15.2	1.3	100	387
	Teachers	0	0	12.2	37.8	48.9	1.1	100	90
	Politicians	0	0.8	18.7	33.3	44.7	2.4	99.9	123
Ascendancy groups	***Immigrants***								
	General public	0.9	7.7	67.5	16.3	3.1	4.6	100.1	326
	Teachers	0	0	39.5	39.5	20.9	0	99.9	43
	Politicians	0	0	42.9	35.7	21.4	0	100	28
	First gen								
	General public	1.7	4.6	54.9	30.1	6.9	1.8	100	173
	Teachers	0	0	19	28.6	52.4	0	100	21
	Politicians	0	0	28	40	32	0	100	25
	Mixed								
	General public	0.8	2.4	51.2	33.1	10.2	2.4	100.1	127
	Teachers	0	0	20	40	40	0	100	25
	Politicians	0	3.7	22.2	33.3	40.7	0	99.9	27
	Natives								
	General public	0.3	1.1	33	48.8	15.8	1.1	100.1	373
	Teachers	0	0	14.7	33.3	50.7	1.3	100	75
	Politicians	0	0	20.2	33.7	43.3	2.9	100.1	104

Source: CIS (1998).

Table 1 also provides some important clues about mechanisms of blockage. First, even though the preferences of the teachers, local politicians and regional parliamentarians are, on the whole, very much in accordance with the existing policy framework, all three of these groups are themselves divided along the lines of language and ascendancy group. Second, the terms of division among Castilian-speaking and Catalan-speaking teachers and politicians are nevertheless significantly more skewed towards the 'all-Catalan' pole, so to speak, than are these terms of division among the general public. In other words, Castilian-speaking teachers and politicians are much more supportive of the current language policy framework than are Castilian-speakers in the general population; but at the same time, these teachers and politicians are much less supportive of the existing policy framework than are their native Catalan-speaking counterparts.

The evidence thus speaks in favour of the existence of two reinforcing processes at work which together certainly contribute to blocking the articulation of the preferences and values of the Castilian-speaking community as a whole. The first is the under-representation of Castilian-speakers among educators in charge of implementing language policies in the schools and among politicians elected to representative institutions in charge of making these policies (Table 2).

Even though, according to the 1998 CIS survey, Catalan-speakers made up only 41% of the general population, they comprised 59.6% of teachers, 62.0% of local politicians and fully 76.8% of parliamentarians. Furthermore, Catalan-speakers were not only predominant in the political class generally; they were also specifically predominant in the ranks of the parties with a significant electoral base of Castilian-speakers—*Iniciativa per Catalunya* (Initiative for Catalonia, IC, a left-wing post-communist formation), the PSC and the PP (Table 3).

Does this make a difference with respect to the positions of the parties who represent Castilian-speakers? If we judge by the opinions of these 'representatives', it would appear that it certainly does—at least for the two parties with a significant Castilian-speaking base that voted in favour of the 1998 LPL (Law of Linguistic Policy). In both IC and the PSC, Catalan-speaking representatives are much more likely to support linguistic policy than are their Castilian-speaking counterparts (Table 4).

Furthermore, the under-representation of Castilian-speakers amongst the elected representatives in the party system is reinforced by the partial assimilation of elected Castilian-speaking representatives into the attitudes and preferences of the

Table 2. Linguistic identity (%)

	Population	Teachers	Local politicians	Parliamentarians
Castilian-speakers	43.0	21.0	20.9	07.1
Bilinguals	16.0	19.3	17.1	16.1
Catalan-speakers	41.0	59.6	62.0	76.8
(*n*)	(744)	(166)	(129)	(56)

Source: CIS (1998).

Table 3. Linguistic identity and party affiliation (%)

		Castilian-speakers	Bilinguals	Catalan-speakers	(*n*)
IC (municipal elections 1999)	Voters	40.3	14.2	45.5	(67)
	Local politicians	27.8	11.1	61.1	(18)
	Parliamentarians	20.0	00.0	80.0	(5)
PSC (regional elections 1999)	Voters	71.5	06.6	21.9	(450)
	Local politicians	29.3	22.4	48.3	(58)
	Parliamentarians	15.0	30.0	55.0	(20)
PP (regional elections 1999)	Voters	81.2	01.6	17.2	(89)
	Local politicians	18.2	36.4	45.5	(11)
	Parliamentarians	00.0	33.3	66.7	(6)

Source: For voters—Institut de Ciències Polítiques i Socials (1999).

Catalan-speaking majority who dominate the political establishment. A look at patterns of subjective self-identification among the population, teachers, and politicians suffices to prove the point. Castilian-speaking, immigrant and first-generation teachers and politicians register significantly more Catalanized identities than do their counterparts in the general population (Table 5).

Finer-grained statistical analysis in the form of odds-ratio simulations reinforces this finding. The ethnolinguistic divide detectable among elites is significantly narrower than it is among the masses; and the terms of division among elites are decidedly more Catalanized. Thus, when we hold other variables at their means, we find that the probability that a local politician whose mother tongue is Castilian and who was born outside of Catalonia registers a predominantly-Spanish identity stands at 4.8%, compared with 48.8% among his/her Castilian-speaking immigrant counterparts in the general population. Interestingly, no similar gaps between Catalan-speaking, native local politicians and their counterparts among the general public can be detected (Tables 6 and 7).

These two mechanisms—under-representation of Castilian-speakers in the region's representative institutions and the partial assimilation of elected Castilian-speakers into the attitudes, identities and preferences of Catalan-speakers, who constitute the hegemonic fraction of the political establishment—together undoubtedly contribute to the rather striking gap between the attitudes and preferences of the voters and those of their elected representatives. The contrasting profiles of the PSC electorate and its representatives are particularly striking in this regard. Not only are socialist representatives much less likely to be non-natives or to have Castilian as their first language than is the socialist electorate, so too are the socialist representatives significantly more likely to register a predominantly Catalan identity, to consider Catalonia a nation, and significantly much less likely to support the presence of Castilian in the educational system or to judge linguistic policy to be excessive or otherwise incorrect (Table 8).

Table 4. Opinion of different linguistic groups in IC and the PSC on the Catalan linguistic policy (%)

		IC				PSC			
		Castilian-speakers	Bilinguals	Catalan-speakers	Total	Castilian-speakers	Bilinguals	Catalan-speakers	Total
Opinion on linguistic policy	Insufficient	16.7	50.0	53.3	43.5	05.0	04.8	33.3	18.8
	Correct	33.3	00.0	13.3	17.4	50.0	66.7	35.9	47.5
	Excessive	00.0	50.0	20.0	17.4	35.0	09.5	17.9	20.0
	Other	50.0	00.0	13.3	21.7	45.0	19.0	12.8	13.8
n		(6)	(2)	(15)	(23)	(20)	(21)	(39)	(80)

Source: own elaboration.

Table 5. Self-identification by linguistic groups and ascendancy groups, elites versus masses (%)

		Spanish	More Spanish	Equally Spanish	More Catalan	Only Catalan	DK/DA	Total	*n*
Mother tongue	***Castilian***								
	General population	27.8	10.7	43.2	13.1	3.6	1.6	100	(1194)
	Teachers	15	8.3	53.3	11.7	6.7	5	100	(60)
	Politicians	3.8	0	71.7	22.6	1.9	0	100	(53)
	Catalan								
	General population	1.3	1.3	20.2	41.8	34.4	1	100	(1346)
	Teachers	0	0	8.8	30.8	59.3	1.1	100	(91)
	Politicians	0	0	24	28.8	44.8	2.4	100	(125)
Ascen-dancy groups	***Immigrants***								
	General population	38.7	12.6	36.5	5.8	3.1	3.4	100.1	(780)
	Teachers	23.8	7.1	54.8	7.1	7.1	0	99.9	(42)
	Politicians	7.1	0	67.9	17.9	7.1	0	100	(28)
	First generation								
	General population	8.4	7.2	54.8	22.5	6.2	1	100.1	(418)
	Teachers	0	4.8	47.6	33.3	14.3	0	100	(21)
	Politicians	0	0	60	24	16	0	100	(25)
	Mixed								
	General population	4.6	6.2	30.3	37.1	20.2	1.7	100.1	(307)
	Teachers	0	4.2	29.2	33.3	33.3	0	100	(24)
	Politicians	0	0	50	26.9	23.1	0	100	(26)
	Natives								
	General population	1.8	1.4	21.3	40.9	33.6	1	100	(1239)
	Teachers	0	0	8	32	60	0	100	(75)
	Politicians	0	0	22.1	33.7	44.2	0	100	(104)

Source: CIS (1998).

Table 6. Simulation of ordinal logit model predicting self-identification

	Immigrants	First generation	Mixed	Natives
Probability that an individual considers him/herself exclusively or predominantly Spanish				
Castilian	0.4880	0.3431	0.2225	0.1355
Bilingual	0.2715	0.1696	0.1006	0.0578
Catalan	0.1272	0.0739	0.0419	0.0234
Probability that an individual considers him/herself equally Spanish and Catalan				
Castilian	0.4199	0.5006	0.5248	0.4829
Bilingual	0.5224	0.5089	0.4356	0.3301
Catalan	0.4738	0.3782	0.2694	0.1751
Probability that an individual considers him/herself exclusively or predominantly Catalan				
Castilian	0.0922	0.1563	0.2527	0.3816
Bilingual	0.2061	0.3215	0.4638	0.6122
Catalan	0.3991	0.5479	0.6887	0.8015

Source: CIS (2001)

Table 7. Simulation of ordinal logit model predicting self-identification

	Immigrants	First generation	Mixed	Natives
Probability that a local politician considers herself exclusively or predominantly Spanish				
Castilian	0.0480	0.0323	0.0215	0.0143
Catalan	0.0116	0.0077	0.0051	0.0034
Probability that a local politician considers herself equally Spanish and Catalan				
Castilian	0.7661	0.7110	0.6350	0.5438
Catalan	0.4933	0.3948	0.3028	0.2238
Probability that a local politician considers herself exclusively or predominantly Catalan				
Castilian	0.1858	0.2568	0.3434	0.4419
Catalan	0.4951	0.5975	0.6921	0.7728

Source: own elaboration.

Table 8. The contrasting profiles of the PSC electorate and its representatives

	PSCelectorate	PSC local politicians	PSC parliamentarians
% that is immigrant or first generation	67.2	35.0	30.0
% whose first language is Castilian	67.0	41.7	30.0
% that registers a predominantly Catalan identity	24.6	43.1	40.0
% that considers Catalonia a nation	22.4	61.7	70.0
% that prefers for school to be taught *at most* half in Catalan	66.9	31.7	30.0
% that judges linguistic policy to be excessive or otherwise incorrect	56.8	36.7	25.0
(*n*)	(539)	(59)	(20)

Source: For electorate—CIS (1998; 2001)

Discussion and Conclusion

This paper has provided strong evidence that the Catalan party system effectively blocks the articulation of the preferences and interests of large segments of Catalan society—especially, working-class Castilian-speakers; and the mechanisms by which such effective blockage has been achieved include the under-representation of Castilian-speakers in the region's representative institutions and the partial assimilation of elected Castilian-speakers into the attitudes and preferences of Catalan-speakers, who constitute the hegemonic fraction of the political establishment.

These findings are of theoretical interest both for scholars of nationalism and for scholars of empirical democratic theory, especially those focused on comparative political elites and comparative party systems. For scholars of nationalism, the success of Catalan political elites in maintaining a high degree of political consensus in favour of nation-building policies, and thus their ability to 'keep a lid' on the articulation of opposition to these policies as a salient axis of party competition in the region's political arena, despite the relative starkness of the region's underlying ethnolinguistic divide, is well worth noting. For it suggests that positions of power in hierarchically organized party structures and highly coveted representative posts are crucial sites that can, in some circumstances, be captured by nationalist sympathizers. Such sympathizers can then use their strategic location to structure the terms of political contestation in such a way as to effectively exclude opposition to nation-building policies; and, in so doing, they can effectively contribute to the construction of the 'nation' (i.e. the victory of the nationalist project) by 'setting the agenda' and implementing policies from the top down, despite lagging levels of popular support. The representative-democratic political arena thus can be a crucial site for building the nation, since 'political supply' need not reflect current societal 'demand', but rather can serve to silence certain demands, privilege others, and shape the contours of future ones. In other words, it can emerge as a relatively autonomous, privileged site for the construction of ideological hegemony, not only through the mobilization of nationalist core constituencies, but also (perhaps even more importantly) through the de-mobilization of potentially anti-nationalist constituencies (Lustick, 1993).

For scholars of empirical democratic theory, the significant gaps between elites and 'masses' in terms of ethnolinguistic backgrounds, cultural identities, linguistic practices, and political preferences, along with the reflection of median-elite preferences in extant nation-building policies, all lend credence to the main contention of theorists, such as Schumpeter (1942) that, at least in some circumstances, 'political supply' is relatively autonomous from, and can shape, societal demand. More precisely, the existence of the two mechanisms here posited converges with the arguments of those 'neo-elitist' theorists who stress how the political arena can be captured by supporters of certain policy agendas, and how opposition to those agendas can thus be effectively marginalized, for better (Higley and Burton, 2006) or for worse (Lewis, 2001). By contrast, the evidence here cuts against those versions of 'neo-elitist' theory that lead us to expect political elites to be more polarized than their respective constituencies (McAllister, 1991; Jennings, 1992)—since, in the case at hand, political elites turn out to be less polarized than the general public, consistently more supportive of nation-building policies than their respective constituencies across the political spectrum.

Moreover, the use of direct comparisons of survey responses of political elites and those of the general public helps overcome problems associated with the fact that public opinion surveys not only measure but also *manufacture* public opinion (Jackman, 1998); and, in so doing, it contributes to the reinvigoration of a strand of literature that aims to measure gaps between elites and 'masses' with a level of precision sufficient to provide robust empirical evidence capable of adjudicating among rival interpretations and hypotheses (Lindblom, 1990; Zaller, 1992).

Finally, it must be stressed that the mechanisms of 'blocked articulation' identified here provide a powerful and parsimonious, but by no means complete, explanation for the significant gaps between public opinion, on the one hand, and elite preferences as well as public policy, on the other. In particular, this analysis emphasizes the limits to Catalan nationalist hegemony at the level of popular identities, cultural practices, and policy preferences. Nevertheless, it is obvious there are strong ideological obstacles to mobilizing and publicly articulating resistance by Castilian-speaking workers to the Catalan nation-building project—most powerful among these, widespread beliefs about the prospects for intergenerational social mobility being associated with knowledge of the Catalan language, as well as widespread beliefs about the defence of the Spanish language and culture being associated with memories of Francoist oppression. Both such widespread beliefs, which can be measured, plausibly contribute to the delegitimization and demobilization of resistance by potential Spanish-speaking constituencies and, therefore, to the achievement and perpetuation of a certain degree of regional-nationalist hegemony.

Likewise, this study emphasizes mechanisms of blocked articulation operative in political parties in Catalonia and in the dynamics of supply-side competition in the Catalan party system. However, the existence of additional mechanisms of blockage operative in the parties and the party system at the level of the whole of Spain cannot be ignored. Indeed, the ideological proclivities and the coalitional strategies of the Socialist Party elites, the multi-dimensional structure of competitive space in the consolidated Spanish party system, as well as the frequent dependence of central governments of both centre-left and rightist persuasion upon support from Catalan nationalists to maintain governing majorities in the Spanish Congress are important features to take into account.

Notes

[1]The five main political forces with consistent representation in the Catalan Parliament (and in the Spanish *Congreso de Diputados*) have been, from left to right: the ex-communist and eco-socialist *Iniciativa per Catalunya* (IC); the social-democratic *Partit dels Socialistes de Catalunya* (PSC-PSOE); the 'radical' nationalist *Esquerra Republicana de Catalunya* (ERC); the conservative and 'moderate' nationalist *Convergència i Unió* (CiU); and the Spanish-right *Partido Popular* (PP). In every regional election since the devolution of powers in 1980, the two political formations with the most votes and most representatives have been CiU and the PSC. From 1980–2003, CiU governed the region; between 2003 and 2010 it was governed by the so-called *tri-partit*, consisting of the PSC, in coalition with the ERC and IC; and, since 2010, it has been governed again by CiU.

[2]Primary and secondary school teachers of social sciences, humanities, and language (168), local politicians (131), and parliamentarians (56).

[3]In forthcoming research, including a new wave of interviews with Catalan political elites, we intend to bring this comparison up to date.

References

Aja, E. (1999), *El Estado Autonómico: federalismo y hechos diferenciales*. Madrid: Alianza Editorial.

Barrera González, A. (1985), *La dialéctica de la identidad en Cataluña*. Madrid: Centro de Investigaciones Sociológicas.

Boix Fuster, E. (1993), *Triar no és trair. Llengua e identitat entre els joves de Barcelona*. Barcelona: Edicions 62.

Bourdieu, P. (1991), Identity and Representation: Elements for a Critical Reflection on the Idea of a Region, *Language and Symbolic Power*. Cambridge: Polity Press.

Brubaker, R. (1996), *Nationalism Reframed: Nationhood and the National Question in the New Europe*. Cambridge: Cambridge University Press.

Budge, I. and McDonald, M. (2006), Choices Parties Define: Policy Alternatives in Representative Elections, 17 Countries 1945–1998, *Party Politics*, Vol.12, No.4, pp.451–466.

Caminal, M. (1998). *Nacionalisme i partits nacionals a Catalunya*. Barcelona: Empuries.

Castells, M. (1997), *The Information Age: Economy, Society and Culture*. Volume II: *The Power of Identity*. Oxford: Blackwell.

CIS (1998), *Uso de lenguas en comunidades bilingües: Cataluña*. No.2298, Madrid: CIS.

CIS (2001), *Situación social y política de Cataluña*. No.2410. Madrid: CIS.

Colomer, J. (1986), *Cataluña como cuestión de Estado*. Madrid: Tecnos.

Conversi, D. (1997), *The Basques, the Catalans and Spain: Alternative Routes to Nationalist Mobilization*. London: Hurst and Company.

Dahl, R. (1971), *Polyarchy*. New Haven: Yale University Press.

De la Calle, L. and Miley, T. J. (2008), Is There More Assimilation in Catalonia than in the Basque Country? Analysing Dynamics of Assimilation in Nationalist Contexts. *European Journal of Political*, Research, No.47, pp.710–736.

Delgado Ruíz, M. (1998), *Diversitat i integració. La lògica de les identitats a Catalunya*. Barcelona: Editorial Empúries.

Departament de Cultura (1998), *Enquesta sobre política lingüística i sobre l'aplicació de la Llei 1/1998*. Barcelona: Generalitat de Catalunya.

Deutsch, K. and Foltz, W. (1963), *Nation-Building*. New York: Atherton Press.

Direcció General de Política Lingüística (2008), *Estadística d'usos lingüístics*. Available at http://www.idescat.cat/cat/societat/usoslinguistics.html (accessed 6 December 2012).

Guibernau, M. (1999), *Nations without States: Political Communities in a Global Age*. Cambridge: Polity Press.

Higley, J. and Burton, M. (2006), *Elite Foundations of Liberal Democracy*. Lanham, Md: Rowman and Littlefield.

Institut de Ciències Polítiques i Socials (1999), *Sondeig d'opinió Catalunya*. Barcelona: ICPS.

Jackman, S. (1998), Pauline Hanson, the Mainstream, and Political Elites: The Place of Race in Australian Political Ideology, *Australian Journal of Political Science*, Vol.33, No.2, pp.167–186.

Jennings, K. (1992), Ideological Thinking among Mass Publics and Political Elites, *Public Opinion Quarterly*, Vol.56, No.4, pp.419–441.

Lago, I., Torcal, M. and Ramón Montero, J. (2007), The 2006 Regional Election in Catalonia: Exit, Voice, and Electoral Market Failures, *South European Society and Politics*, Vol.12, No.2, pp.221–235.

Laitin, D. (1987), Linguistic Conflict in Catalonia, *Language Problems and Language*, Planning, Vol.11, No.2, pp.129–147.

Levin, J. (2010), The Role of Language in Nationalist Movements: Explaining the Origins and Development of Catalan and Basque Language Policies in Education. MPhil Dissertation, Department of Politics and International Relations, University of Oxford.

Lewis, J. (2001), *Constructing Public Opinion: How Political Elites Get What They Like and Why We Seem to Go Along with It*. New York: Columbia University Press.

Lindblom, C. (1990), *Inquiry and Change: The Troubled Attempt to Understand and Shape Society*. New Haven: Yale University Press.

Linz, J. (1985), De la crisis de un Estado unitario al Estado de las Autonomías, in F. Fernández Rodríguez (ed.), *La España de las Autonomías*. Madrid: Instituto de Estudios de Administración Local.

Linz, J. (1993), State Building and Nation Building, *European Review*, Vol.1, No.4, pp.355–369.

Lustick, I. (1993), *Unsettled States, Disputed Lands*. New York: Cornell University Press.
Marfany, J.-L. (1995), *La cultura del catalanisme: El nacionalisme català als seus inicis*. Barcelona: Editorial Empúries.
Martínez-Herrera, E. (2002), From Nation-building to Building Identification with Political Communities: Consequences of Political Decentralisation in Spain, the Basque Country, Catalonia and Galicia, 1978–2001, *European Journal of Political Research*, Vol.41, No.4, pp.421–453.
Matas Dalmases, J. (1995), *Els alts càrrecs: Polític i administració a la Generalitat de Catalunya*. Barcelona: Generalitat de Catalunya.
McAllister, I. (1991), Party Elites, Voters and Political Attitudes: Testing Three Explanations for Mass-Elite Differences, *Canadian Journal of Political Science*, Vol.24, No.2, pp.237–268.
Miley, T. J. (2006), *Nacionalismo y política lingüística: el caso de Cataluña*. Madrid: Centro de Estudios Políticos y Constitucionales.
Miliband, R. (1989), *Divided Societies: Class Struggle in Contemporary Capitalism*. Oxford: Clarendon Press.
Orizo, F. A. and Roque, M.-À. (2001), *Los catalanes en la encuesta de valores*. Madrid: Ediciones SM.
Pallarés, F. (ed.). (2000), *Eleccions i Comportament Electoral a Catalunya 1989–1999*. Barcelona: Ed. Mediterrània.
Pallarés, F. and Font, J. (1995), *The Autonomous Elections in Catalonia (1980–1992)*. Barcelona: Institut de Ciències Polítiques i Socials.
Przeworski, A. and Sprague, J. (1986), *Paper Stones: History of Electoral Socialism*. Chicago: University of Chicago Press.
Pujol, J. (1976), *Inmigració: problema y esperança de Catalunya*. Barcelona: Terra Nova.
Requejo, F. (2005), *Multinational Federalism and Value Pluralism: The Spanish Case*. New York: Routledge.
Riba, C. (2000), Voto dual y abstención diferencial: Un estudio sobre el comportamiento electoral en Cataluña, *Revista Española de Investigaciones Sociológicas*, No.91, pp.59–88.
Rodríguez, M. J., Güell, M. and Telmer, C. (2007), Intergenerational Mobility and the Informative Content of Surnames, CEPR Working Paper, No.6316.
Schumpeter, J. (1942), *Capitalism, Socialism, and Democracy*. New York: Harper and Row.
Secretaria de Política Lingüística (2008), *Les llengües a Catalunya: resultats de l'Enquesta d'usos lingüístics a la població 2008*. Barcelona: Generalitat de Catalunya.
Shafir, G. (1995), *Immigrants and Nationalists. Ethnic Conflict and Accommodation in Catalonia, the Basque Country, Latvia, and Estonia*. Albany: State University of New York Press.
Solé, C. and Alarcón, A. (2001), *Llengua i economia a Catalunya*. Barcelona: Institut d'Estudis Catalans.
Termes, J. (1999), *Les arrels populars del catalanisme*. Barcelona: Editorial Empúries.
Viçens Vives, J. (1961), *Cataluña en el siglo XIX*. Madrid: Rialp.
Vila i Moreno, F. X. (1993), *Transmissió dels idiomes en les parelles lingüísticament mixtes*. Barcelona: Generalitat de Catalunya, Departament de Cultura.
Woolard, K. (1989), *Double Talk: Bilingualism and the Politics of Ethnicity in Catalonia*. Stanford, Ca: Stanford University Press.
Woolard, K. (1997), Between Friends: Gender, Peer Group Structure and Bilingualism in Urban Catalonia, *Language in Society*, Vol.26, No.4, pp.533–560.
Woolard, K. (2003), 'We Don't Speak Catalan Because We Are Marginalized'; Ethnic and Class Connotations of Language in Barcelona, in R.K. Blot (ed.), *Language and Social Identity*. Westport: Praeger.
Zaller, J. (1992), *The Nature and Origins of Mass Opinion*. New York: Cambridge University Press.

The Jacobin Republic and Language Rights. Ethnolinguistic Mobilizations in France

ALISTAIR COLE* & JEAN-BAPTISTE PAUL HARGUINDÉGUY**

*Cardiff University, Cardiff, UK, **Public Law-Political Science, Universidad Pablo de Olavide, Seville, Spain

ABSTRACT France is usually considered as the symbol of cultural unification and homogeneity. It is commonly (and, in part, correctly) assumed that the process of political centralization in France profoundly shaped the language preferences of citizens. Nevertheless, sociological surveys reveal a tension between the Jacobin Republican drive for uniformity and a more fine-grained empirical reality in the field of the governance of regional languages. Through the comparison of three case studies (Corsica, Brittany and Picardy), this paper reveals that the defence of lesser-used languages and regional dialects has produced an asymmetrical form of ethnolinguistic mobilization by social movements and political parties, which has been more or less credible depending on processes of institutionalization, actor-accommodation and the official recognition of the lesser-used language in question. Through focusing on the specific case of regional languages, the article leads us to examine not only the recent transformations of the French language policy model, but also to reconsider the nature of the contemporary French state.

Introduction

The European nation-state building process generally consisted of the state imposing one language in order to favour the constitution of a uniform nation (Blattberg, 2006: 597; Patten, 2007: 15). The French case, where resolute state action set out to homogenize cultural differences as early as the nineteenth century, is exemplary of these broader trends. That this process of cultural homogenization partially failed has received little attention from scholars. Empirical research demonstrates, however, both the emergence of a variety of ethnolinguistic social movements and territorial representative institutions mobilizing in support of a new deal for regional languages and the taking into consideration of this issue by the central government (Poignant, 1998; Cerquiglini, 2003). This article takes as its starting point this apparent contradiction between the Jacobin Republican myth and a more fine-grained empirical reality in the field of the governance of regional languages. Through focusing on the specific case of regional languages, the article leads us to examine not only the recent transformations of the French language policy model, but also to reconsider the nature of the contemporary French state.

Language policy in France has generated an important political literature over the last 30 years. Beyond the pioneer investigations led in the early 1980s by French sociologists on regionalist social movements (Bourdieu and Boltanski, 1981: 2; Touraine *et al.* 1981; Bourdieu, 1982), three main academic dimensions can be identified in the current literature about language policy. First, political scientists focusing on the process of state (and nation) building have written interesting accounts about how state languages converted regional languages into lesser-used languages and, in turn, provoked a reaction against the dominant language (Allardt, 1979: 44; Hobsbawm, 1996: 85; Clairis *et al.*, 1999; Fishman, 2000; Klatter-Folmer and van Avermaet, 2001; Romaine, 2002: 194). Second, authors who adopt a regional studies' perspective have stressed the link between identity, language policy and nationalism, demonstrating that the promotion of regional identities and minority languages does not always support separatist aims (Loughlin, 1985: 101; Judge, 2000: 44; Timm, 2001: 104; Cole and Williams, 2004: 554; Harguindéguy and Ballester, 2007: 89). Finally, political theorists working on theories of justice argue that Western states have established three types of relationship with minority languages: a neutral stance in respect of all languages consistent with Rawlsian liberal theory (United States); the active promotion of all threatened languages in line with communitarian claims (Canada, Spain, Belgium); or the active support of just one language (or a few languages) based on a republican perspective thought to facilitate the political participation of all citizens (France) (Taylor, 1985; May, 2001; Kymlicka and Patten, 2003).

Is France the exception which confirms the rule of multiculturalism? While a majority of European states are currently implementing cultural devolution processes, France is sometimes portrayed as the only country to restrict the linguistic rights of its 'minorities'. Such a vision belies a more complex situation, where there is a mix of a republican-inspired linguistic uniformity and empirical adaptability to uneven territorial situations and social mobilizations. The formalization of a number of hypotheses might allow us to capture this variation. The first of these we label *ethnolinguistic mobilization.* Though it is perfectly correct to argue that France remains a centralized state from a linguistic viewpoint, the state has been forced to adapt as a result of the mobilization of ethnolinguistic activists since the late 1960s. Our second hypothesis is that of *international diffusion*; the active policy of European institutions and international organizations in favour of the constitutional recognition of regional languages has gradually forced the French government to become more receptive to regional language claims. Our third hypothesis we label as that of *asymmetrical endogenous institutionalization*; the adaptability of public officials to the cause of language activists has produced different levels of institutionalization according to place. Though a degree of asymmetry exists, the progressive opening of the linguistic opportunity structure still largely depends on the position of the central state and not on an abstract process of either Europeanization or convergence to international norms.

We propose to assess these hypotheses through a Weberian approach in terms of linguistic market, defined as a competitive space where linguistic entrepreneurs struggle to impose their language (Bourdieu, 1982; Solé and Alarcón, 2001). Our case studies are Corsican, Breton and Picard; three lesser-used languages selected because of their different numbers of speakers and of their distinctive modes of mobilization.[1] The article is divided into two parts. In section one, we discuss the evolution of the French institutional framework for the governance of language issues. In section two, detailed case studies of Corsican, Breton and Picard are presented. In a brief conclusion, the hypothesis will be revisited in order to provide a consistent explanation of this phenomenon.

A Centralized Language Policy

France is usually considered not only as the archetype of a centralized nation-state, but also as the paradigmatic case of language centralization. This centralizing ambition was not initially directed against regional languages. During the *ancien regime*, the core aim of the language policy implemented by Monarchy consisted in substituting Latin with French in order to reinforce the influence of the Crown on administrative issues, an objective reached in 1539 with the *Ordonnance de Villers-Cotterêts* (Elias, 1982).

The rupture provoked by the French Revolution profoundly modified the linguistic aims of the state. An ambitious programme of language centralization was launched from the capital in order to promote the French language—the symbol of modernity—against local *patois*—that is regional languages assimilated to Reaction, the Church and the Aristocracy. One century later, linguistic unification was virtually complete. A decisive step towards French linguistic hegemony was reached under the Third Republic, through an important effort realized in the field of education (the Ferry laws of 1881 and 1882) when regional languages were banned from schools. The supremacy of French was facilitated by the diffusion of French newspapers, military conscription, the construction of a modern Paris-centred transportation system, the standardization of weights and measures and the emergence of a modern capitalist market centred in Paris. By the First World War, French had imposed itself as the main language of the nation-state in the cities, with regional languages finally succumbing to French during the Second World War in rural areas (Weber, 1977). Meanwhile, the first laws promoting 'dialectal languages' were adopted in 1941 and 1942 by the pro-fascist government led by *maréchal* Pétain. Such laws were inspired by the ideology of the reactionary Catholic monarchist and anti-Semitic writer Charles Maurras, a defender of provincial traditions of 'real France' (as opposed to 'legal France' created by the institutions of the Revolution). For many, that historical episode made illegitimate the defence of these tongues after the war (Barral, 1974: 911–939).

Nowadays, Republican institutions adopt a deeply ambivalent attitude towards regional languages. They sometimes tolerate non-French languages but rarely do they totally support them. One sign of toleration was offered in 2001, when the General Delegation for the French Language of the Ministry of Culture was transformed into the General Delegation for the French Language *and the Languages of France*. On the other hand, the French government has ratified neither the UNESCO

Convention against discrimination at school (1980) nor the Council of Europe's Charter for Regional and Minority Languages (1992) (Wright, 2000: 414). French language regulation strictly forbids activities which could endanger the monopoly of the French language: it re-affirmed the importance of French in 1992 adding that "the language of Republic is French" to the Constitution as article two and, in 1994 through the Toubon Law, implementing measures to defend French against English in the public sphere. However, the Jacobin *ethos* of French deputies is progressively evolving towards a more liberal position since a new article (75-1) was introduced in the French constitution in 2008. This article states "regional languages belong to the France's cultural heritage". Time will tell if this article will break the current institutional deadlock.

Seventy-five regional languages or dialects are spoken in France, two-thirds of which are used in the French overseas territories (Figure 1; Table 1). As ethnic statistics are forbidden in France, it is extremely difficult to get trustworthy data about the number of regional language speakers and their language skills. Until recently the different surveys were usually based on the declaration of interviewees, and not on any grammatical or objective exercises. Moreover, these surveys used small samples and their results were sometimes contradictory. This situation has been slowly changing as local and regional institutions have gathered more robust data since the late 1990s.

Figure 1. Linguistic areas of regional languages in France.
Source: Harguindéguy and Cole (2009: 939–967).

Table 1. Estimated number of speakers of regional languages in continental France and Corsica

Languages	Estimated number of speakers (in France as a whole)	Language skills (according to the survey, the criteria of evaluation are different)		
Alsatian	900 000	43% speak	33% understand	
Francique	400 000	–		
Flemish	30 000	1% speak well	2% can understand	
Breton	172 000	13% speak fluently	7% speak and understand quite well	
Oïl languages	204 000	–		
Franco-Provencal	70 000	–		
Catalan	126 000	49% speak	16% understand	
Occitan	3 000 000	45% understand	25% speak	6% write
Corsican	150 000	81% understand	64% speak	57% read
Basque	72 000	9.1% speak	21.4% understand	

Source: Berthoumieux and Willemsma, 1998; Fusina, 2000; Cole and Williams, 2004: 554–579; Euromosaic, 2007; 2008; Conseil régional Rhône-Alpes/Institut Pierre Gardette, 2009; Aménagement linguistique dans le monde, 2010; Office pour la langue et la culture d'Alsace/ED Institut, 2012; Vice-ministère de la politique linguistique/Office public de la langue basque, 2012).

A number of important laws have been passed in the post-war period that gave some form of official recognition to regional languages. The first one was the Deixonne Law (11 January 1951) which allowed regional languages to be taught for three hours a week in public schools. In 1975, the Haby Law confirmed this provision and listed the regional languages which could be legally taught; these were Breton, Basque, Catalan, the Oc languages and Corsican, a core to which other languages were added during the 1970s. In 1982, following Mitterrand's election as President in 1981, the Savary decree allowed private, 'contracted-in' schools to teach regional languages if public schools were not able to do so. Following this reasoning, in 1995 the Ministry of National Education granted a 'contracted-in' status to those associative schools (such as *Diwan* in Brittany) which taught through the medium of the regional languages, the method known as *immersion*. Moreover, the 1995 decree also legalized the teaching of regional languages throughout the whole educational system, namely in monolingual (French) and bilingual (French and regional language) schools, belonging to public, private or associative sectors. This provision was extended to the French overseas territories with the decree of 13 December 2000. At the same time, the Deixonne Law was repealed in 2000, and replaced by the new article 4 of the Education Code which extended the right to teach regional languages to the whole educational programme (from primary to secondary school). One year later, the Academic Councils for Regional Languages were created to oversee this new system.

If the case of education is one of developing capacity, outside of the classroom the space for developing and using regional languages is limited. First—and however peculiar this might seem—the Villers-Cotterêts decree still regulates the use of language in the administrative and legal systems. French remains the only written language allowed in official correspondence, though regional languages can be used by citizens if civil servants understand them. In some regions, road signs and postal addresses can also be written in the vernacular language if the state administrations give their agreement. Since the 22 July 1982 and 1 August 2000 laws, moreover, public broadcasters can diffuse programmes in regional languages, a practice promoted by the local stations of *Radio France*'s network, the *Radio France Outre-mer* company and the TV channel *France 3.*

Comparing Ethnolinguistic Mobilizations in France

This study demonstrates that ethnolinguistic movements exist in France, but the policy repertoires used by their activists differ greatly from one case to the other. In the main body of the article, the cases of the Corsican and Breton languages and the Picard regional dialect are investigated, comparing their history and context, dissemination and institutionalization, as well as the territorial coalitions that advocate supporting the language and the ambivalence of French state actors to the whole issue area.

Ethnolinguistic Mobilizations in Corsica: From the Street to the Parliament

Corsica is a Mediterranean island situated 200 km from the French coast, close to Sardinia. The 294 118 inhabitants of the island (in 2008) are the product of successive invasions. Genovese invaders occupied Corsica from 1000 to 1755 when local rebel troops led by Pasquale Paoli declared the independence of the island and established their own constitution in Corte. The Treaty of Versailles (1768) and the defeat of Paoli's followers at the battle of Ponte-Novu in 1769 made official the transfer of control of the island from the Genovese administration to the French state, a situation that has persisted ever since.

The Corsican language is a Romanic tongue spoken mainly in the island. It is divided into three main groups: Northern Corsican (*lingua suprana*), Central Corsican (*lingua mizana*) and Southern Corsican (*lingua suttana*) that all can be used by Corsican speakers in the name of the 'polynomic Corsican' concept. Such linguistic tolerance slowed the taking into account of Corsican as a language *per se* by the Deixonne Law until 1974, as it was considered a mere dialect of Italian—the traditional majority language of the island under the Genovese invasion. Indeed, the process of 'gallicization' of the island was initially conceived as a fight against Italian; the diffusion of French with respect to Corsican only became a consistent policy from the Second World War (Jaffe, 1999; Blackwood, 2004: 133). By that time, the Corsican people faced an original situation of triglossia by speaking Corsican, Italian and French at the same time.

According to a study carried out in 1995, 81% of local inhabitants understand Corsican, 64% speak it and 57% are able to read it (Fusina, 2000); such percentages are higher in the north than in the south of Corsica because of the higher isolation of rural areas in the south. This means that Corsica is not in a situation of French quasi-monolingualism—like those lesser-used languages surviving in other French regions—but rather in a position of diglossia (referring to the different competences of local speakers in French and in Corsican). The long-term trend has been for a weakening of the Corsican language environment and transmission. Economic under-development and emigration have strongly modified the traditional mechanisms of familiar transmission of Corsican since the 1940s. Some 500 000 Corsican people now live in mainland in France and approximately one million live outside French borders (most of them in Italy). The arrival of foreign populations (especially those French people expelled from Algeria from 1957 onwards) has contributed to the marginalization of Corsican as a language, henceforth principally used by the popular classes and by older people in rural areas (INSEE, 2004).

Corsican language issues were, historically speaking, intrinsically linked to nationalism and the core demands of nationalist political parties. The call for independence by the founding father of Corsican nationalism, Pasquale Paoli, and the cultural renewal promoted in the 1920s by the *Partitu Corsu d'Azione* constitute the intellectual base of the nationalist movement. During the 1960s different clandestine nationalist groups began to organize violent actions to catch the attention of continental mass media. From the Aléria affair, led by the Corsican Regionalist Action in 1975, to the elimination of the prefect Erignac in 1998, by one of the numerous subdivisions of the Front for the National Liberation of Corsica created in 1976, Corsican nationalists have tried to maintain political pressure on successive French governments, by using all means including political violence. Though some nationalists have continued to justify the use of violence, most of the island's political actors prefer non-violent participation through the devolved institutions.

Language policy in favour of Corsican has had an impact, however, especially in the field of education, where activists were mobilized early on to defend the teaching of classes 'in' and 'of' Corsican in public schools. As a result, most public primary schools offer lessons in Corsican for a minimum of three hours a week; a minority of them (around 60) operates a completely bilingual curriculum for their students. Corsican lower secondary (*collèges*) and upper secondary (*lycées*) schools may also organize an optional course in 'regional culture and languages' and offer Corsican as a second or third language. Upon passing their baccalaureate, university students can enter the Faculty of Corsican language created by the University of Corte (Fusina, 2000). Corsican language courses are freely available for adult learners. Outside of the network of public (state) schools, some nursery and primary schools belonging to private cultural associations teach the Corsican language through the linguistic *immersion* system (also used in Brittany, for example). Nevertheless, their number is very limited and they are tending to be replaced by public centres of linguistic immersion directly managed by the regional government (in Savaghju, Loretu di Casinca and Bastia). However important these incremental measures might be, they are a far cry from the initial ambition of the Assembly of Corsica's nationalist deputies to make learning Corsican obligatory throughout the public educational system.

Outside of the education field, the presence of Corsican remains marginal. Though, in theory, citizens can use Corsican in their relations with public administration and in their dealing with the legal system, such use is rare as this provision depends upon state officials speaking Corsican too. The use of Corsican in the mass media is also patchy. The public broadcaster *Radio France* diffuses various programmes in Corsican via its local public radio station *France Bleue Frequenza Mora*, along with five news bulletins a day. Some private radio stations also use Corsican as the only language for their programmes (stations such as *Alta Frequenza*, *Voce Nustrale* and *Radio Golfe*). In relation to television, the local public channel *France 3* broadcasts documentaries and TV shows in Corsican, as well as a news report entirely in Corsican diffused at different times of the day. The local and regional press dedicate little editorial space to Corsican (*Corse Matin*, *La Corse*) and those few newspapers and magazines entirely published in Corsican are closely monitored by the nationalist movements (*Scontru*, *U Ribombu*, *Arritti*, *Rigiru*). Finally, theatre and cinema in Corsican remain insignificant despite the efforts realized in this sector.

Corsica is ruled by a special statute of autonomy voted in 1982 and modified in 1991 and 2002. Since the 13 May 1991 Law, Corsica is no longer a normal French region but a Territorial *Collectivité* of the Republic, which is usually consulted by the French National Assembly when dealing on issues related with Corsica. Under this special statute, an Executive Council is elected (and can be vetoed) by an Assembly which represents the interests of the whole of the island. Decision-making powers are shared, however, with the two *départements* (Southern Corsica and Northern Corsica), which have important prerogatives in fiscal and cultural issues, including the promotion of Corsican. In a referendum in July 2003, Corsican electors narrowly voted to reject (50.98% voted 'no') the proposal of former Minister of Interior Nicolas Sarkozy to merge the actual regional assembly and the two departmental councils into a unique regional government, a development which would appear to have arrested the rise of the Corsican nationalists.

The operation of the devolved institutions in Corsica has been shaped by the embedded insular traditions of traditional clientelism (between local bosses and the citizen) and clandestine behaviour, notably in the form of extortion and the traffic of ballot papers. In many respects, Corsican devolution has strengthened the role of these traditional *notables* as brokers between local interests and central state representatives. The role performed by the nationalists is deeply ambivalent. Though the Corsican nationalists gained popularity by condemning the collusion between *notables* and the French state, they were also prompt to bargain on measures such as the amnesty of 'political prisoners' by the penal administration. Both the traditional *notables* (in the centre-right *Union pour la Majorité Parlementaire*/Union for a Popular Movement, or the centre-left *Parti socialiste-Radicaux de gauche*/Socialist Party/Leftist Radicals and the nationalists are divided into clans and irredentist movements, making any agreement between them highly problematic. The convergence of material interests between *notables* and nationalists, however, led to the creation of a proportional representation system in elections to the Corsican assembly, with two rounds of voting, facilitating the representation of most nationalist families, as well as the main French parties governed by local *notables*.

The Corsican Assembly has demonstrated itself not only to be an efficient instrument for channelling radical nationalist movements, but also has provided an institutional foundation for promoting language rights (Collectivité territoriale de Corse, 2007). The promotion of the Corsican language has become linked with the development of decentralized political institutions that have acquired a degree of autonomy in the cultural domain. In 1983, one of the first measures adopted by the first Assembly was to vote in favour of the compulsory teaching of Corsican in public schools, a decision immediately rejected by the Socialist Prime Minister Mauroy. Corsica's elected representatives have continued to press for obligatory language teaching and for the recognition of Corsican as a second official language alongside French. The Culture Committee of the Assembly is at the forefront of this process of language advocacy. After having invested approximately €10 million in cultural projects since its creation, the Assembly finally adopted in 1999 a plan for the development of Corsican. The failure of enhanced political autonomy in the July 2003 referendum has not impacted unduly on the demands for more language rights, which are broadly shared across the political spectrum, including amongst the 'French' parties.

Language rights form one part of a broader nationalist campaign. The visibility of the Corsican language today is due in part to the success of the nationalist campaigns of the 1980s, when language activists daubed road signs written in French with Corsican. The French authorities ultimately conceded that road signs should be written in French and in Corsican. The existence of decentralized institutions, the Assembly and the Executive Council, with a degree of autonomy on cultural issues, has provided an institutional basis for such linguistic advocacy. One of the main claims of the nationalists still remains the promotion of Corsican language, understood as the "language of the nation" (Blattberg, 2006: 597); this explicitly appeared in the political programme of the four nationalist deputies elected to the Assembly in 2010. The principal nationalist groups represented are *Rinnovu*, *Strada Dritta*, *Accolta Naziunale Corsa* and *Corsica Nazione Indipendente* grouped into the same parliamentary group (*Corsica Libera*) piloted by Jean-Guy Talamoni. These parliamentary groups are still strongly connected to nationalist associations and play an important role in the Assembly by representing them and supporting their proposals (for example by tabling an amendment on 26 June 1992 to make Corsican a co-official language).

Though nationalist parties claim a monopoly of the defence of the Corsican language—and 'Corsicaness'—the two biggest state-wide parties (Union for a Popular Movement and Socialist Party/Leftist Radicals) also support this language policy through their active work within the Territorial *Collectivité*. The Assembly and the Executive Council, under different political complexions and using a variety of procedures (such as questions, motions and the common declaration) have actively backed these initiatives in favour of the Corsican language. The pro-Corsican consensus was demonstrated in the negotiation of the current State Region Plan (2007–13), by article seven of the 22 January 2002 Law on Corsican at school or the cross-border co-operation operational programmes monitored with Italian authorities and Sardinian schools through the Interreg programme. One recent example of this cross-partisan pro-Corsican consensus was provided by the ninth amendment tabled by the alliance of nationalist parties, *Unione Naziunale*, during the elaboration of the Regional Training Plan; this amendment, which advocated the creation of a specific diploma for teaching Corsican culture and language in public schools, received the unanimous backing of the French parties (Third extraordinary sessions of 29 and 30 June 2006).

Is there any linkage between the feeling of Corsican identity and support for the language? Few relevant surveys have been carried out in France since 'ethnic statistics' are forbidden by law, but the findings of the Euromosaic poll in 2002 shed an interesting light on the link between "Corsicaness" and "attitude *vis-à-vis* Corsican language" (Institut de Sociolingüística Catalana, 2002). This poll demonstrates that 88% of people living in Corsica feel profoundly Corsican and only 11% do not feel especially Corsican. From another perspective, 59% consider themselves as French when 41% reject this identity. This survey also shows that local identities (hamlet, island) are more important than state and European identities. Lastly, 84.2% of people encourage the institutional backing of Corsican language, 91.2% think that Corsica would not be the same without the Corsican language and 89.8% are convinced that it is essential Corsican children learn to speak Corsican.

The relations between the defenders of Corsican and the French state are deeply ambiguous. On the one hand, the territorial state has traditionally reached local arrangements with the main *notables* of the island, and has provided financial assistance for core Corsican cultural projects through the State-Region Plans. Specifically, as part of the 2007–13 State-Region Plan, the French state is co-financing Corsica Region's Training Plan 2007–13, which contains provisions for an ambitious linguistic regeneration policy. On the other hand, 30 years of bargaining have not greatly modified the position of the French state about regional languages. For example, in 1991, the Constitutional Council, the highest constitutional authority in France, rejected the concept of "a Corsican nation within the French nation". Moreover, in 2002, the Council accepted the principle of public funding for the Corsican language only on condition that it remains optional, not obligatory.

The Corsican case benefits from a comparative advantage in respect of the other regional languages in France in terms of number of speakers and the public dissemination of Corsican. The institutional structure of the island favours the promotion of Corsican, as demonstrated by the different initiatives implemented by the Territorial *Collectivité*. The latter constitutes an important political resource for local ethnolinguistic networks by giving them official representative channels. Yet, the French state's linguistic policy has evolved very slowly and the non-recognition of international regulation for promoting regional languages strongly limits the efficiency of local arrangements.

The Pro-Breton Movement: Can Civil Society Save a Threatened Language?

One of the most distinctive regions of France, Brittany, has a strong sense of its specific position within French society. Formerly an independent Duchy (from 818 to 1532), then a French province with special prerogatives (1532–1789), reduced for long to being a collection of disparate *départements* before becoming an administrative then political region, modern Brittany is a French region with a difference. Brittany is sometimes taken as a litmus test for the health of regional identity within France. In historical terms, Brittany corresponds well to one of those regions identified by Rokkan and Urwin (1982), in which the development of regional consciousness is a function of economic dependency and the persistence of a strong cultural identity.

Though the symbols of statehood have long disappeared, the region retains many distinctive characteristics, not least that of the Breton language, a Celtic language that is separated from the British Isles from which it originated. The spoken Breton of lower (western) Brittany is fairly homogenous along a north-east–south-west line from Guingamp to Quimper. The three *départements* where Breton is spoken are Côtes d'Armor, Morbihan and Finistère. The first two are traditionally Breton speaking in the west, and Gallo speaking in the east. To the east and south-east of the Guingamp–Quimper line lies the romance-speaking Upper Brittany, where the Gallo dialect is still spoken alongside French. However, beyond these dialectical differences, Breton has also been standardized, as have other many regional languages. 'Neo-Breton' progressively rose during the late-twentieth century and rapidly became a regional *koine* among younger speakers.

At the turn of the twentieth century there were around 1.5 million Breton speakers according to Broudic (1983) and Gourvil (1952). Humphreys (1991: 96) has estimated that by 1962 this figure had dropped to *c*. 686 000 speakers. In the Economic and Social Research Council-funded survey conducted in 2001, around 200 000 people claimed to speak Breton fluently, to which we can add 100 000 who are able to speak and understand quite well (Cole, 2004). This represents 10%, at most, with any sort of Breton language competency. Whether these figures are accurate or not is another matter; it is notoriously difficult to establish accurate figures from polling data in this area. Some previous estimates of the number of Breton speakers have been too low, because some native Breton speakers are reluctant to reveal their fluency to pollsters. However, these figures would appear to be broadly consistent with other recent surveys (Office de la Langue Bretonne, 2004). The demographic and age structure profile is challenging for the future of the language. The majority of Breton speakers is to be found in the upper age groups—the average age being *c*. 65-years old—and is likely to live in a narrow triangle in the westernmost part of Brittany (inland Finistère and the western half of the Cotes d'Armor). The only finding offsetting this rather sombre picture lies in the somewhat broader geographical spread of Breton, along with evidence that there is some revival of Breton amongst the younger age groups. More pupils are today following Breton language classes at school than ever before and adult training courses in Breton are thriving (Mercator, 2003; Ti ar vro Kemper/ Office de la Langue Bretonne, 2006).

Though Breton language activists aspire to ensure the survival of Breton as a *langue de société*, it is no longer the primary means of communication outside of activist circles. The revival of the language can be attributed in part to the success of Breton language activists in creating a Breton medium movement and in mainstreaming the Breton language. The first Breton language school was opened in Finistère in 1977 by a group of Breton language activists, determined to provide a Breton-medium education for their own children. These parents created the *Diwan* association. The first few *Diwan* schools were concentrated in the nursery and primary sector, with one, then several *collèges*, and, finally, a *lycée* in Carhaix. By 2002, *Diwan* alone was in charge of the education of 2768 pupils (2127 in primary and maternal schools, 504 in *collège* and 137 in the *lycée*). In 2005, more than 10 000 pupils were receiving part of their education through the medium of Breton, either in the *Diwan* 'immersive' schools or in the bilingual sections of the Catholic (*Dihun*) or Public (*Div Yezh*) schools. In its language plan of 2004, the Brittany Regional Council targeted 20 000 pupils by 2010 (Conseil Régional de Bretagne, 2004). To argue that these schools have reversed linguistic decline would be excessive. But there has emerged a new generation of fluent Breton speakers that is beginning to enter into professional life.

With the 1982 laws on decentralization, the regional councils have become important co-financers of cultural policy, including that of regional languages. French local and regional authorities have a general administrative competency, allowing them to develop policies in all areas except those specifically forbidden by the law. The law thus opens a policy space within which local and regional authorities can develop more or less proactive policies. In the case of Brittany, most of the drive towards the institutionalization of a language policy has come from the Brittany Regional Council. The Region provides grants to the Breton-medium *Diwan* schools and to a host of Breton cultural movements. The 1994–99 State Region Plan created a publishing company—*Tes*—whose responsibility is to disseminate teaching and learning materials in Breton (books, but also CD-R). The creation of the Breton Language office (*Ofis ar Brezhonneg*) in 1999 was a milestone in terms of institutional development and linguistic communication. *Ofis ar Brezhonneg* is not, strictly speaking, a language board with statutory powers. Its tools are those of persuasion rather than constraint. But it has been very active in promoting the cause of the Breton language, notably through its commercial technical translation service, its bilingual signposting activities (for local government, hospitals, schools), its website and the advice it provides to firms, agencies and individuals on all Breton language issues. In November 2004, the Socialist-led majority issued the first ever Breton language development plan, containing an ambitious range of targets for linguistic development.

The activities of local authorities have complemented those of the region. Sympathetic local councils have adopted a range of measures to promote the language. These range from the symbolic (signposting) to the eminently practical, such as providing buildings for *Diwan* schools, or, in two precise cases, providing land for a Breton enterprise zone (Carhaix) or a Breton cultural district (Quimper). Councils sometimes provide buildings for adult training courses in Breton, which have traditionally been provided on a voluntary basis. Councils also provide buildings for continuing education (evening classes) and professional training in Breton by organizations such as *Stumdi* and *Roudour*. At the most symbolic level, bilingual signposting has become the norm in areas such as Cornouailles and Trégor, where there are sizeable populations of Breton speakers. Local and departmental authorities have pursued this policy vigorously, notwithstanding run-in with local prefects and administrative authorities. Bilingualism has also become fashionable in economic circles. Associations of Breton employers, such as *Produit en Bretagne*, contain within their midst the most important employers in the main economic sectors in Brittany: transport, agro-alimentary, electronics, banks and insurance companies. Breton businesses will employ the language if it is in their commercial interest to do so and some banks in Breton-speaking areas have begun to employ Breton-speaking clerks to deal with clients. But they will equally oppose the language if seen to threaten their core interests.

If there is no comparable mainstreaming of the Breton language within Brittany to that which was witnessed in Wales or Catalonia, the embattled status of the Breton language gives its advocates cohesion in adversity. If it is impossible to detect any single actor, a constellation of individuals, semi-official agencies and voluntary associations can be identified, gravitating for the most part around the regional council. These actors form part of a language advocacy coalition that draws its strength not so much from institutionalization, as from shared beliefs and from the capacity to mobilize the powerful Breton cultural movement. This advocacy coalition includes actors within local and regional authorities, semi-autonomous agencies, such as the Breton Language Office and the cultural federations regrouped in the Brittany Cultural Institute and the Brittany Cultural Council. A very dense tissue of cultural associations exists in Brittany. The main cultural federations—such as *Dastum* or *Tiarvro*—certainly consider themselves part of the broader Breton movement (*Emsav*). These associations operate at various levels. Most are local, limited to a locality or a town (such as the myriad of Breton music groups and dance troops in Quimper). Some operate at a departmental level. Few are genuinely regional, but the most important are regrouped into two major federations at the all-Brittany level: the Brittany Cultural Institute (ICB), based in Vannes and the Brittany Cultural Council (CCB) in Rennes.

The vitality of the cultural movement stands in contrast to the emasculation of a genuine political regionalist movement. There are two main explanations for the weakness of the regionalist movements. First, Bretons have refused to support in meaningful numbers any movement that calls into question Brittany's belonging to the French Republic, a conformist sentiment that is reflected in the modest scores obtained in elections by the Breton Democratic Union (UDB) and the smaller Breton regional or autonomist parties. Second, the political opportunity structure in the French Fifth Republic is so resolutely Paris-centric that Breton forces have adapted accordingly. There is an underlying consensus amongst the 'French' parties to defend Breton interests to the outside world and limit political conflict. This consensual model is broadly shared within Breton public opinion, where there is a high degree of trust in the regional council, a belief that the region defends Brittany's interest well in other arenas and a preference for the region over other arenas in many important areas of public policy (Cole and Loughlin, 2003: 265). There is limited support for political autonomy and it was impossible to identify a real constituency for combining language, identity and the demand for enhanced territorial political institutions along the lines of the nationalist parties in Wales or Catalonia. Breton-style identity politics (including the politicization of language) were discredited by the collaborationist activities of a pro-Nazi minority of Breton activists during the Second World War.

The French state has itself adopted an ambivalent attitude towards demands for Breton cultural and linguistic specificity. On the initiative of President Giscard d'Estaing, in 1977 the French state, the main local authorities and the regional cultural associations signed the Brittany Cultural Charter, which recognized the cultural specificity of Brittany and provided for the establishment of new institutions to promote Breton culture and history. Most innovatively, the 1977 charter incorporated the five regions of historic Brittany, including the Loire-Atlantique (in the Pays de la Loire Region). This episode demonstrated that the French state would, in certain circumstances, recognize the validity of Breton cultural claims and treat Brittany rather differently from other regions. By including Loire-Atlantique, the state accorded some legitimacy to the idea of historic Brittany.

The ambivalence of French state actors is particularly visible in the field of education. On 29 April 2001, an agreement was signed between the socialist Education Minister Jack Lang and Andrew Lincoln, President of the *Diwan* association of Breton-medium schools. Under the terms of the agreement, the 29 *Diwan* schools (and their 2300 pupils) would enter the public education service, an offer that was opened to other immersive language education movements (representing Basque, Corsican, Occitan, Catalan, Creole and Alsatian). For the most part, these schools already enjoyed 'contracted-in' status, rather similar to the denominational (mainly Catholic) schools. Becoming part of the public education service would give the *Diwan* schools much greater financial security. In return, they would be expected to teach as much French as other schools in the state sector. This episode demonstrated opposition to the *Diwan* agreement came from movements generally associated with the left. The national teaching unions were mainly against, as were the lay pressure groups (especially the *Comité National d'Action Laïque*, powerful amongst teachers) and the main parents association, the *Fédération Nationale des Parents d'Élèves*. The Education ministry itself was clearly divided between a sympathetic minister, on the one hand, and a reluctant top administration on the other. Within the Rennes Academy, opinions also ranged, predictably, between firm support and barely veiled opposition. In November 2001, the Council of State advised against implementing the ministerial decree; in 2002 the Constitutional Council declared the agreement to be unconstitutional, on account of the immersive teaching method whereby the language of instruction would be Breton, not French.

Most Bretons support the Breton language in so far as it gives symbolic expression to Breton culture, but even Breton speakers themselves are very reluctant to link language use with institutional preferences. While the Breton cultural movement has been very powerful, it has built its regional advocacy on cross-partisan support and has avoided politicizing language issues. If there is wide-scale general support for the Breton language as a symbol of the region's past, interventionist public policies to sustain Breton are not widely advocated. There is only minority support for policy solutions that have been experimented or openly envisaged in Wales or Catalonia, such as reserving employment for bilingual speakers or training more Breton speakers to take up new employment opportunities. The case of education is particularly illuminating. According to the *Efficience 3* survey, while over 80% support the principle of Breton language teaching as a good thing, hardly any (7%) believe that learning Breton should be obligatory at school. On the other hand, measures perceived to assist the Breton cultural movement are widely approved, with strong majorities agreeing that Breton-medium cultural associations and media should be part-financed from public funds.

Oïl Languages and Picard: In Search of Institutional Backing

The Picard is used in a small territory including parts of France (Nord-Pas-de-Calais and Picardie regions) and Belgium (Province of Hainault), spoken by a small minority of a total population of 5.8 million inhabitants based in the French area. This is a Galloroman language belonging to the Oïl group (Oïl means 'yes', as '*oui*' in French) which is the main language group in northern France (traditionally opposed to the southern

Oc group) that includes other languages, such as French (*Francien*), *Poitevin-Saintongeais*, *Franc-Comtois*, Walloon, Norman, Gallo and *Bourguignon-Morvandieu*. Nowadays, French is the most spoken language of that group. Because of their geographical and linguistic proximity with French, the remaining Oïl languages are sometimes considered erroneously as dialects of French. Picard itself includes many subdivisions, depending on the area taken into account. Subsequently, *Amiénois*, *Vimeu-Ponthieu*, *Vermandois*, *Thiérache*, *Beauvaisis*, *Ch'timi* (also called *Ch'ti*) and the different types of *Lillois*, *Borain*, *Rural Arthésien* and *Boulonnais* are the multiple dialects of the same linguistic system. Beyond this scientific exposure, the Picard language is usually known as Picard in the Picardie region and as *Ch'ti* in the Nord–Pas-de-Calais region; it is also called *patois* in a negative sense as if it was a subordinated dialect of French.

Picard faces the situation of being an ultra-minority language. Though there are very few statistics about the use of Picard, in one estimate only 12% of inhabitants of the Picardie and Nord–Pas-de-Calais regions regularly use it. Among these regions, the most Picard-speaking departments are the Somme (27.3%), the Pas-de-Calais (22.2%) and the Nord (10%), with far more speakers than in Oise or in Aisne (3%) (Blot *et al.*, 2004).

Picard has suffered as much from its inherent linguistic properties, as from the structure of opportunities regulating different lesser-used languages in France. Its first problem is the absence of common orthographical rules which makes Picard dependent upon French and Walloon linguistic norms. The writing system based on Walloon—the so-called Feller-Carton method—remains the most used by researchers. The second limit to Picard development lies in its weak social prestige with respect to French. Though Picard was employed by influential authors during the Middle Ages (see, for example, the Sequence of Saint Eulalie or the books of Adam de la Halle), it became a spoken-only language whose use was limited to the popular classes and to speakers over 60. Moreover, the French nation-building process had a crucial influence on Picard, which was progressively absorbed by the French language and finally generated a sort of 'regional French' with a specific accent and a peculiar vocabulary following the syntax of the dominant language. Such a situation of 'unipolar diglossia' means that local speakers usually meet some difficulties in distinguishing between French and Picard (Dawson, 2004: 287).

In addition, Picard has not benefited from comparable institutional or political support to either Corsican or Breton. In the field of education, for example, Picard is not recognized by the Deixonne Law and cannot be systematically taught despite the efforts undertaken by some associations of Picard promotion in primary schools like the *Veillées Patoisantes de Tourcoing*. More systematic opportunities are available at the level of higher education. The University of Picardie has been particularly active in supporting research about the evolution and dissemination of Picard, while the universities of Amiens and Villeneuve d'Ascq also organize courses on Picard culture and language for their students.

The weak ethnolinguistic mobilization in favour of Picard must be qualified. It is superior to the rest of Oïl languages though weaker than in Corsica, for instance. Yet, the public existence of Picard relies on the goodwill of speakers, who are generally reticent to speak it in public. Very few entertainment or artistic projects are entirely led in Picard, exceptions being the puppet show of the Louis Richard Theatre company or the stand-up show organized by the comedian Dany Boon in 2005. When such public performances take place, they are enthusiastically supported by the audience. In the same way, some journals and magazines use Picard as a first language, like in the case of the Web monthly *Ch'Lanchron*.

The institutional resources of Picard in France are extremely weak. This situation contrasts with the Belgian case, where the French-speaking community recognizes Picard as a regional endogenous language like Walloon, *Gaumais* (Lorraine), *Champenois* and *Francique* through the 24 December 1990 Decree. On the French side, however, Picard has no legal recognition. This lack of institutional backing has partly determined the actual policy repertoire (or 'non-repertoire') of Picard defenders. As elsewhere, the decentralization reforms of the early 1980s provided some institutional support. The regional councils of Picardie and Nord–Pas-de-Calais have implemented an embryonic linguistic policy which still lacks consistency, in part because of the particular situation of Picard, divided into two administrative regions. The Office for Language and Culture of Picardie, funded by the Picardy Regional Council, backs many activities like the translation of books into Picard or the organization of the festival *Ches Wèpes*. In the Nord–Pas-de-Calais Region, on the other hand, there is no specific policy for promoting Picard. The recent creation of the annual Interregional Days for Picard may be the first stone for a common language policy grouping French and Belgian actors.

Unlike in Corsica or Brittany, there are no powerful regionalist parties that advocate specifically Picard values or defend the Picard language. In contrast with the Corsican case especially, the defence of Picard is a linguistic issue. Picard counts its strongest supporters amongst a number of cultural associations ruled by the 1901 Law. Some of these associations act as a lobby at the local and regional levels, with the *Union Tertous*, *Ch'Lanchron* or *Insanne* arguing in favour of the recognition of Picard as a regional language, a status that would allow it to be taught in public schools under the Deixonne Law. These associations have some institutional backing—mostly from the Picardie Region—but they are territorially fragmented and operate in a less favourable environment in the neighbouring Nord–Pas-de-Calais region. Unlike in Corsica or Brittany, there is a weak coalition of institutions and social movements mobilized for the defence of the regional language. Ethnolinguistic activists are condemned to organize themselves without a consistent leadership and with few institutional resources at their disposal. The low level of institutionalization of this network is compounded by the lack of a strong feeling of belonging of the inhabitants of Picardie and Nord–Pas-de-Calais (in 1998, 20% of Picards feel 'very proud' of their region, against 62% in Brittany and 55% on Corsica) (Dargent, 2001: 787).

In this specific case, there is no state policy in respect to Picard since it has not still been recognized as a regional language. In addition, the cursory attention paid by citizens to this issue reveals that this 'non-policy' has been accepted by potential Picard speakers themselves. Only the report written in 1999 by Cerquiglini (2003), from the National Institute of French Language for the Ministry of Culture, mentions the Picard and Oïl languages as languages *per se* and not as mere dialects of French. These conclusions were then used by the High Council of Languages and Cultures from France which now publishes some information about Picard on its website.

In sum, despite a relatively high level of acceptance among citizens and some ethnolinguistic activists grouped into associations, Picard crucially lacks institutional backing or the support of powerful social movements or regionalist/nationalist parties. The contrast with Belgium, where Picard is recognized as a language in its own right, is stark. The fate of Picard confirms the need for political and institutional resources to underpin language revival. A lack of institutional capacity or political support deepens the isolation of regional language supporters in France.

Conclusion

Is France the exception which confirms the rule of multiculturalism? France is sometimes portrayed as the only country to restrict the linguistic rights of its 'minorities'. Such a vision belies a more complex situation, where there is a mix of a republican-inspired linguistic uniformity and empirical adaptability to uneven territorial situations and social mobilizations.

We argued above that the formalization of a number of hypotheses might allow us to capture this variation. One such hypothesis was that of *international diffusion*, whereby the active policy of European institutions and international organizations in favour of the constitutional recognition of regional languages would gradually encourage the French government to become more receptive to regional language claims. Far from being convinced of the weight of extraneous variables, we found little evidence that European institutions or international organizations, or even notions of best practice, have had much impact upon the receptivity of French government to regional language claims. The progressive opening up of the linguistic opportunity structure still largely depends on the position of the French state and not on an abstract process of externally driven convergence.

We identified two broad domestic-level categories; ethnolinguistic mobilizations and asymmetrical endogenous institutionalization. In practice, it is difficult, analytically or empirically, to distinguish between social movement and institutional explanations, though logically speaking the former precede the latter. Though remaining centralized from a linguistic viewpoint, the French state has been forced to adapt as a result of the mobilization of ethnolinguistic activists since the late 1960s, which has gradually produced a pattern of uneven and imbalanced institutionalization. The recognition of regional languages in the constitution in 2008 marks the high point of this gradual, incremental process of linguistic institutionalization. Our evidence from Corsican, Breton and Picard cautions in favour of the need to accommodate place-specific explanations within any framework of analysis. The untidy reality is one where place-specific social movements are more or less effective in mobilizing the support of broad advocacy coalitions and in achieving degrees of institutionalization. The result is a pattern of *asymmetrical endogenous institutionalization*, where the adaptability of public officials to the cause of language activists has produced different levels of institutionalization according to place.

The strongest combination of social movement and institutional variables is in Corsica, where ethnolinguistic movements have mobilized support within and beyond nationalist parties and dispose of an easy access to political representative institutions through the Corsican Assembly which constitutes a powerful instrument to 'Corsicanize' French public administration. At a lower level, Breton activists remain a marginalized social movement represented by a dense network of associations without strong connections with Breton nationalists—who are themselves a very small group anyway—but with some access to and support within regional representative institutions. Lastly, the case of Picard demonstrates that some ethnolinguistic coalitions fail even to reach the minimal level of institutionalization. The logical corollary is that Picard remains a vague concept that very few people can identify as a language and a culture *per se*.

France faces an ambivalent situation. While the republican *credo* of the state remains profoundly anchored in Jacobin traditions and public declarations, local arrangements between decentralized authorities and ethnolinguistic activists have modified linguistic practice in an incremental 'Girondin' manner. This unsung aspect of the Republic deserves to be recognized. The evidence presented in this article, whereby a place-specific policy of recognizing linguistic pluralism has gathered momentum alongside the persistence of an overarching centralizing ideological framework, demonstrates the flexibility of the French Republic.

Note

[1]This investigation is based on a series of structured interviews, a mass survey in Brittany in 2001 and on an inquiry of secondary literature and grey literature carried out between 2001 and 2006. This comparative investigation received the financial backing of the post-doctoral programme of the French *Centre National de la Recherche Scientifique* and, for the Breton case, of the UK Economic and Social Research Council (grant number L215292007). This article was finalized as part of the Leverhulme Trust's International Network on 'Territorial Governance in Western Europe: between capacity and convergence' (IN-2012-109).

References

Allardt, E. (1979), Implications of the Ethnic Revival in Modern, Industrialized Society. A Comparative Study of the Linguistic Minorities in Western Europe, *Comentationes Scientarum Socialum*, No.12, pp.44–63.

Aménagement Linguistique dans le Monde (2010), available at www.tlfq.ulaval.ca/axl/ (accessed 20 August 2012).

Barral, P. (1974), Idéal et pratique du régionalisme dans le régime de Vichy, *Revue Française de Science Politique*, Vol.24, No.5, pp.911–939.

Berthoumieux, M. and Willemsma, A. (1998), *The Occitan Language in Education in France*. Leeuwarden: Mercator-Education. Available at http://www.mercator-research.eu/fileadmin/mercator/dossiers_pdf/occitan_in_france.pdf (accessed 20 August 2012).

Blackwood, R.J. (2004), The Gallicization of Corsica: the Imposition of the French Language from 1768 to 1945. *Language Policy*, Vol.3, No.2, pp.133–152.

Blattberg, C. (2006), Secular Nationhood? The Importance of Language in the Life of Nations, *Nations and Nationalisms*, Vol.12, No.4, pp.597–612.

Blot, D., Eloy, J.-M. and Rouault, T. (2004), La richesse linguistique du nord de la France, *Profils INSEE Nord-Pas-de-Calais*, No.1.

Bourdieu, P. (1982), *Ce que parler veut dire. L'économie des échanges linguistiques*. Paris: Fayard.

Bourdieu, P, and Boltanski, L. (1981), Le fétichisme de la langue, *Actes de la Recherche en Sciences Sociales*, No.3, pp.2–17.

Broudic, F. (1983), *Al Liberterien hag ar brezoneg – 'Brug': 1913–1914*. Brest: Brud Nevez.

Cerquiglini, B. (2003), *Les langues de France*. Paris: Presses Universitaires de France.

Clairis, C., Costaouec, D. and Coyos, J.-B. (eds) (1999), *Langues et cultures régionales de France. Etat des lieux, enseignement, politiques*. Paris: L'Harmattan.

Cole, A. (2004), *Devolution and Decentralization in Wales and Brittany, 2001–2002*, UK Data Archive, No.4802.

Cole, A. and Loughlin, J. (2003), Beyond the Unitary State? Public Opinion, Political Institutions and Public Policy in Brittany. *Regional Studies*, Vol.37, No.3, pp.265–276.

Cole, A. and Williams, C. (2004), Institutions, Identities and Lesser-used Languages in Wales and Brittany, *Regional and Federal Studies*, Vol.14, No.1, pp.554–579.

Collectivité territoriale de Corse (2007), *Plan de développement de l'enseignement de la langue et de la culture corse et son apprentissage tout au long de la vie*. Bastia: AGEP.

Conseil Régional de Bretagne (2004), *Projet de budget primitif*. Rennes: Conseil Régional de Bretagne.

Conseil régional Rhône-Alpes/Institut Pierre Gardette (2009), *Etude Fora. Francoprovençal et occitan en Rhône-Alpes*. Lyon. Available at http://www.ddl.ish-lyon.cnrs.fr/aalled/Telechargeable/bert_2009_francoprovencal_rapport_FORA.pdf (accessed 20 August 2012).

Dargent, C. (2001), Identités régionales et aspirations politiques: l'exemple de la France d'aujourd'hui, *Revue Française de Science Politique*, Vol.51, No.5, pp.787–806.

Dawson, A. (2004), L'patois s'apprind tout seu: les pièges de l'enseignement du picard, *Ela: études de linguistique appliquée*, No.136, pp.487–498.

Elias, N. (1982), *The Civilizing Process. Power and Civility*. New York: Pantheon Books.

Euromosaic (2007), *Catalan in France*. Institut de Sociolingüística Catalana. Available at http://www.uoc.edu/euromosaic/web/document/catala/an/i5/i5.html (accessed 20 August 2012).

Euromosaic (2008), *Le Flamand en France*. Research Centre of Multilingualism. Available at http://www.uoc.es/euromosaic/web/document/neerlandes/fr/i1/i1.html (accessed 20 August 2012).

Fishman, J. A. (ed.). (2000), *Can Threatened Languages be Saved*. Clevedon: Multilingual Matters.

Fusina, J. (2000), *The Corsican Language in Education in France*. Leeuwarden: Mercator-Education. Available at http://www.mercator-research.eu/fileadmin/mercator/dossiers_pdf/corsican_in_france.pdf (accessed 20 August 2012).

Gourvil, F. (1952), *Langue et littérature bretonnes*. Paris: Presses Universitaires de France.

Harguindéguy, J.-B. and Ballester López, M. (2007), Acción colectiva y enseñanza de las lenguas regionales en Francia (1951–2006). Una primera aproximación, *Revista Española de Ciencia Política*, No.16, pp.89–108.

Harguindéguy, J.-B. and Cole, A. (2009), La politique linguistique de la France à l'épreuve des revendications ethnoterritoriales, *Revue Française de Science Politique*, Vol.59, No.5, pp.939–967.

Hobsbawm, E. (1996), Are all Tongues Equal? Language, Culture and National Identity, in P. Barker (ed.), *Living as Equals*. Oxford: Oxford University Press.

Humphreys, H. L. (1991), The Geolinguistics of Breton, in C.H. Williams (ed.), *Linguistic Minorities, Society and Territory*. Clevedon: Multilingual Matters.

INSEE (2004), Langue corse: réception, transmission et pratique, *Économie corse*, No.105.

Institut de Sociolingüística Catalana (2002), Corsican Language use survey Euromosaic survey', *Euromosaic*. Barcelona: Universitat Oberta de Catalunya. Available at http://www.uoc.es/euromosaic/web/document/cors/an/e1/e1.html (accessed 20 August 2012).

Jaffe, A. (1999), *Ideologies in Action: Language Politics in Corsica*. Berlin: Mouton de Gruyter.

Judge, A. (2000), France: One State, One Nation, One Language, in S. Barbour and C. Carmichael (eds), *Language and Nationalism in Europe*. Oxford: Oxford University Press.

Klatter-Folmer, J. and van Avermaet, P. (eds) (2001), *Theories on Maintenance and Loss of Minority Languages*. Munster: Waxmann.

Kymlicka, W. and Patten, A. (eds) (2003), *Political Theory and Language Rights*. Oxford: Oxford University Press.

Loughlin, J. (1985), A New Deal for France's Regions and Linguistic Minorities, *West European Politics*, Vol.8, No.3, pp.101–113.

May, S. (2001), *Language and Minority Rights*. Harlow: Longman.

Mercator-Education (2003), *The Breton Language in Education in France*. Ljouwert: Mercator-Education.

Office de la Langue Bretonne (2004), *Charte d'Ya d'ar Brezhoneg*. Carhaix: Office de la Langue Bretonne.

Office pour la langue et la culture d'Alsace/ED Institut (2012), *L'Alsace en version originale*. Strasbourg. Available at http://www.olcalsace.org/sites/default/files/documents/etude_linguistique_olca_edinstitut.pdf (accessed 20 August 2012).

Patten, A. (2007), Theoretical Foundations of European Language Debates, in D. Castiglione and C. Longman (eds), *The Language Question in Europe and Diverse Societies*. Portland: Hart Publishing.

Poignant, B. (1998), *Rapport sur les langues et cultures régionales*. Paris: Ministère de la Culture.

Rokkan, S. and Urwin, D. W. (1982), *Economy, Territory, Identity. Politics of Western European Periphery*. London: Sage.

Romaine, S. (2002), The Impact of Language Policy on Endangered Language, *International Journal on Multicultural Societies*, Vol.4, No.2, pp.194–212.

Taylor, C. (1985), *Human Agency and Language*. Cambridge: Cambridge University Press.

Ti ar vro Kemper/Office de la Langue Bretonne (2006), *Le Bilinguisme dans votre commune*. Carhaix: Office de la Langue Bretonne.

Timm, L. (2001), Ethnic Identity and Minority Language Survival in Brittany, in C. O'Reilly (ed.), *Language, Ethnicity and the State,* tome I. London: Palgrave.

Touraine, A., Dubet, F., Hegedus, Z. and Wievorka, M. (1981), *Le pays contre l'Etat, luttes occitanes*. Paris: Seuil.

Vice-ministère de la politique linguistique/Office Public de la Langue Basque (2012), *V° Enquête Sociolinguistique. Euskadi, Navarre et Pays Basque Nord.* San Sebastián. Available at http://www.mintzaira.fr/fileadmin/documents/Aktualitateak/fr_Euskal_Herria_inkesta_soziolg_2011_20120716.pdf (accessed 20 August 2012).

Weber, E. (1977), *Peasants into Frenchmen. The Modernizat8ion of Rural France*. London: Chatto and Windus.

Wright, S. (2000), Jacobins, Regionalists and the Council of Europe's Charter for Regional and Minority Languages, *Journal of Multilingual and Multicultural Development*, Vol.21, No.5, pp.414–425.

Ethnopolitical Mobilization without Groups: Nation-Building in Upper Silesia

MAGDALENA DEMBINSKA

Department of Political Science, University of Montreal, Quebec, Canada

ABSTRACT Ethnolinguistic political mobilization has spread throughout the post-communist area. However, it is unclear whether it has been accompanied by a strengthening of group boundaries. This paper examines the nation-building process of unrecognized Silesians in Poland. It explores the mobilization strategies used by Silesian ethnopolitical entrepreneurs in their quest for regional autonomy and recognition of their language and group. I argue that the increase in the number of self-declared Silesians and the successful institutionalization of a Silesian national category have not led to mass national consciousness. Due to structural transformations and transnational processes, Silesians display multidimensional fluctuating identifications, which suggest the absence of a sense of national groupness.

Introduction

Since the fall of communism in 1989, instances of ethnolinguistic political mobilization have proliferated in Central Europe and Eurasia. However, it is unclear whether they have led to stronger ethnic group boundaries. In order to determine whether this is the case, this article examines the ethnopolitical movement of Silesians in Poland. While they are not recognized by the state as a minority group distinct from the majority Polish nation, Silesian entrepreneurs demand territorial autonomy and official recognition of what they claim are the Silesian language and nation. They have managed to put their cause on the agendas of both the state and the European Union. Since the 2002 census, which included an open question on subjective nationality and, surprisingly, found that Silesians were the largest minority in Poland, Silesian organizations have succeeded in (a) increasing the number of self-identified Silesians in the 2011 census, (b) reopening the 2005 Minorities Law in order to add Silesians to the list of recognized minorities, in the category of regional language groups, and (c) forming a regional coalition government in 2010. How have Silesian entrepreneurs managed to institutionalize language as a marker of Silesian identity? Does the increase in the number of self-declared Silesians mean the masses adhere to the elite-driven national project, so that the category is invested with groupness?

This paper shows, first, that, in spite of the state's refusal to officially recognize Silesians as a distinct group, the institutionalization of their "status as [a] partner in the dispute on the issue" (Buchowski and Chlewińska, 2012: 9) and thus of the Silesian identity category has been achieved through an instrumental re-imagination of the Silesian community and a standardization of the Silesian ethnolect, an ethnolect being a written language or unwritten vernacular used by an ethnic group to distinguish itself from others (Majewicz, 1989: 10–13; Kamusella, 2004b: 35). Because of the controversy surrounding the official recognition of Silesian, following Janicki (2009), the term *ethnolect* will be used here in order to avoid attributing a particular status of language or dialect to the Silesian verbal code. Second, it is argued that this national identity category lacks as yet a cohesive groupness—a sense of being a nation. The evidence suggests that achieving mass adherence to the idea of the Silesian nation is complicated in the context of this borderland (at least until 1945 for Upper Silesia) cultural region—Silesian collective identity was shaped by centuries of changing state borders and the penetration of distinct national cultures and traditions (Szczepański, 1997; Wilson and Donnan 1998; Simonides, 2004; Kłoskowska, 2005; Suchocka, 2006; Kurczewski, 2006). The case of Silesia suggests that nation-building in the twenty-first century may be a dynamic unending process, as people tend to acquire multidimensional identities forming ever-shifting layers.

Nations do not appear on the map suddenly. Miroslav Hroch (1993: 6–7), describes the nation-building process as follows:

> Between the starting-point of any given national movement and its successful conclusion, three structural phases can be distinguished, according to the character and role of those active in it, and the degree of national consciousness emergent in the ethnic group at large. During an initial period, which I have called Phase A, the energies of the activists were above all devoted to scholarly enquiry into and dissemination of an awareness of the linguistic, cultural, social and sometimes historical attributes of the non-dominant group ... In a second period, or Phase B, a new range of activists emerged, who now sought to win over as many of their ethnic group as possible to the project of creating a future nation, by patriotic agitation to 'awaken' national consciousness among them ... Once the major part of the population came to set special store by their national identity, a mass movement was formed, which I have termed Phase C.

Silesian nation-building experienced modest A and B phases in the nineteenth and the beginning of the twentieth centuries. It never became a mass movement. Post-1989 structural changes in Poland, however, provided an opportunity to take up phase B again. At the same time, activists were forced to resume phase A, as the dissemination of Silesian national attributes, such as a standardized language and a Silesian historiography, were limited. Despite claims by ethnopolitical entrepreneurs, it is unclear whether ethnolinguistic Silesian mobilization has led to phase C.

This paper separately examines top-down and bottom-up processes of national group formation. Following Brubaker (2006: 10–12), ethnicity and nationality are considered particular identity categories that are invested with 'groupness' by ethnic entrepreneurs who activate identity attributes. The 'politics of categories from above' are first examined, by looking into Silesian entrepreneurs' strategies to institutionalize the Silesian national category. The movement has been seeking to legitimize its cause in the public arena by standardizing its ethnolect and history as a means of reinforcing its position in relation to the Polish state; the latter requires evidence of a distinct culture and language for official recognition. These actions aim to ensure the future existence of "ecological niches, such as schools, in which [the group] can survive and develop" (Brubaker, 2006: 26). However, since category institutionalization does not ensure the strengthening of 'groupness', this article aims to explore how the categorized respond to the categories proposed to them (Brubaker, 2006: 13). Very few studies address societal responsiveness to ethnopolitical mobilization (Stroschein, 2011). If it is accepted that identities are socially (re-) constructed (Young, 2002; Hale, 2004: 466; May *et al.*, 2004: 9; Maíz and Requejo, 2005: 2–5), it should also be accepted that ethnic elite political actions can transform collective identities. Identity is composed of multiple identifications that cumulate, coexist and collide when exposed to different contexts and choices (Hale, 2004). Depending on the needs of the moment, one identification takes precedence over others. Acquisition or crystallization of an identification transforms identity. We can thus observe over time the "fluctuating salience of national identities with respect to other social allegiances" (Hutchinson, 2000: 651). Vural and Rustemli (2006: 330) write:

> Identity fluctuation can be associated with a change in the prevailing components of identity. Such a change constitutes a departure from the crucial component of the existing collective identity leading to partial demotion or even elimination of the official or politically supported component of identity.

The paper argues that the structural changes that occurred after 1989 and the increased political opportunities associated with the opening of political space and the process of transnationalization, limit the capacity for developing a new fixed and bounded national mass 'groupness'—phase C in Silesian nation formation. Traditional Silesian attributes have been transformed and individuals have developed multidimensional, complementary identifications. The Silesian national identification is "occasional" (Kłoskowska, 1995) as other identifications—civic, regional, Polish, German and European—may take precedence depending on the context.

Silesian Identity and the 'Biggest National Minority' in Poland

Silesian is a borderland identity that attaches great importance to the local territory and is formed through a three-way interaction with the majority nations to the east (Poles), to the west (Germans) and to the south (Bohemians/Czechs). In the tenth century, Silesia, inhabited by Western Slavs, was incorporated into Poland, and later was divided between Upper and Lower Silesia. In the twelfth century, Germanic people settled in Lower Silesia. Both Upper and Lower Silesia were transferred to the

Czech Crown in 1348. Czech was established as the official language in Upper Silesia, mainly inhabited by Catholic Slavs, whereas German was spoken in Lower Silesia, which was mostly populated by Protestant Germans. In the mid-eighteenth century, most of Silesia was transferred to Prussia, and a small portion was given to the Austrian Empire. Both empires implemented Germanization policies in the territory. After World War I, Austrian Silesia was divided between Poland and Czechoslovakia; the rest of Upper Silesia was split between Germany (Opole region) and Poland (Katowice region). Polish Silesia was granted territorial autonomy in the 1920 Constitution. Its functioning was much disturbed by opposing visions of two main partisan competitors, the pro-Polish *Sanacja* aiming at Polonization and integration of Silesia within a unitary Poland, and *Chadecja* aiming at fully exercising Silesia's competencies in order to constitute Poland's driving force (Ciagwa, 1988; Bialasiewicz, 2002). The German occupation of Poland in 1939, *de facto* terminated the autonomy by fusing Polish Upper Silesia into the German province of Silesia.

After World War II, almost the entire German portion of Silesia fell under Polish rule. The National State Council (KRN)—nucleus of the Communist government—formally abolished Silesian autonomy in May 1945. Germanization was replaced with Polonization (Mucha, 1997: 31; Linek, 2001). The Polish language became mandatory, with German and Silesian forbidden (Mucha, 1992: 469; Kamusella, 1994: 114). Silesians who were close to the German culture were expelled to Germany (based on the 1945 Potsdam Agreement) or sent to work in camps in the Soviet Union (Szmeja, 2002: 47). Over 3.5 million Germans were expelled from Silesia and from former East Prussia (Bialasiewicz, 2002). The territory was further Polonized through the settlement of Poles expelled from Eastern territories that were incorporated into the USSR (Ruszczewski, 1995; Kochanowski, 2001). Over 1.5 million 'repatriated' Poles, followed by expelled Ukrainians and Rusyns from eastern Poland (Vistula Action) moved into the region. In Upper Silesia alone, as of 1950, 806 800 Upper Silesians remained and 591 300 Polish expellees settled in. In Germany, there were some 800 000 Upper Silesian expellees (Kamusella, 1999: 417). Furthermore, intergovernmental agreements for 'family reunification' allowed over 1 198 000 people, among them 600 000 Upper Silesians, to emigrate to West Germany, between 1955 and 1989 (Kamusella, 1999; Bialasiewicz, 2002). The number of Upper Silesians and their descendants living in present-day Germany is around 1.5 million (Kamusella, 2002). At the same time, subsequent communist governments developed Upper Silesia into the 'Polish Eldorado' where, in the 1970s and 1980s, over a quarter of the entire Polish GNP was generated and where thousands of workers and their families from all parts of Poland settled (Bialasiewicz, 2002). These forced and induced migrations considerably modified the ethnic make-up of the region. Most of the present-day inhabitants arrived after 1945.

Shifting control over Silesian territory and the constant 'second class' status of its native inhabitants, contributed to the development of a Silesian identity (Kamusella, 1994; Szmeja, 2002: 45). They are neither German nor Polish, and they feel considerable resentment against both nations (Gerlich, 1994). However, the borderland context prevented the development of a Silesian high culture that would facilitate the formation of a nation. Silesian scientists and artists, in order to exist, had to resign themselves to identifying as Polish or, more frequently German (Kłoskowska, 2005: 235). That being said, some ethnic mobilization did take place in the nineteenth and the beginning of the twentieth centuries (Sekuła, 2010: 120–122; for language aspects, Kamusella, 2011). For example, in 1849, Jan Gajda suggested the creation of the Silesian League, which would support "matters purely Silesian and promote Silesian nationality" (Pędziwiatr, 2009). Fifty years later, in 1909, the Silesian People's Party was established by Józef Kożdoń and a weekly newspaper was published (Pędziwiatr, 2009). Such examples provide a useful, although scarce, repertoire for present-day ethnic entrepreneurs. In sum, Silesians have a very strong and deeply rooted ethnic conscience; they identify themselves as Silesian in all social situations (Szmeja, 1998: 80). They believe they have their own language and culture, a common history and a territory of origin. Based on these elements, Silesian organizations claim the recognition of the Silesian language and national identity, a demand that contradicts the Polish state's position that Silesians are part of the Polish nation and that their ethnolect is a dialect of the Polish language.

The largest part of the historic Silesian territory is now in Poland and covers three *voïvodships*: Lower Silesia (Dolnośląskie); Opolskie and Śląskie (formerly Katowickie) which both include the territories of historic Upper Silesia. Most (85.8%) self-identified Silesians reside in Śląskie, mainly around the Katowice region (Nijakowski, 2006: 161); it is also here that interwar autonomy was granted (for the history of the regional administrative divisions, see Wódz and Wódz, 2006) and where the present-day Silesian ethnopolitical movement operates. Research conducted in Katowickie/Śląskie (that is within an administrative *voïvodship* limits comprehending the interwar Polish Upper Silesia augmented with non-Silesian historical territories) in 1996 and in 2007, shows the following self-declared identifications: Polish, 63.8% in 1996 and 70.9% in 2007; Polish-Silesian, 18.1% then 9.6%; Silesian,12.4% and 16.8%; German-Silesian, 2.4% and 0.9%; and German, 1.1% then 0.5% (Świątkiewicz, 2005: 94; Kijonka-Niezabitowska, 2009: 95). As mentioned above, the majority of the region's population is not autochthonous, which has direct implications on the ways that Silesian nation-building is constructed. Research also indicates some identity transformation over the period. This most clearly occurred between 2002 and 2011. In the 2002 census, 173 000 Polish citizens identified as Silesian (with some 148 000 in Upper Silesia only). In 2011, 809 000 people declared such an identity, constituting the largest minority in Poland.

In the 2002 census the question on 'nationality' allowed ample space for subjective declarations but only one identification was possible. In 2011, the question was modified. Citizens could declare their first national or ethnic belonging, followed by a second attachment. The preliminary results published in March 2012 show that, of the 809 000 self-declared Silesians, 418 000 gave Silesian as a first attachment, with 362 000 declaring it to be their sole identification; 391 000 chose Silesian as their second identification; 415 000 combined Silesian with Polish identifications (first or second). The increase in self-declared Silesian identification is not surprising. The youngest generation could not speak for itself in 2002 but could do so in 2011 and research among secondary school and college students in 2008 showed that 45.1% identify as Polish, 42% as Polish-Silesian, 6.5% as Silesian and 1.4% as German (Kijonka-Niezabitowska, 2009: 96). It should also be noted that in 2002 and then in 2011 fewer citizens declared themselves of German nationality, while the number of self-declared Silesians grew (Nijakowski, 2006: 151; Skomorowska, 2012). That being said, *such* an increase was unexpected. The remainder of this article explores legitimization strategies 'from above' and the investing of the Silesian national category with history and language. It also investigates whether growing Silesian self-identification is leading to a phase C.

Investing the Silesian National Category with Groupness

Legitimizing the Silesian National Movement in the Public Sphere

At the beginning of the 1990s, Związek Górnośląski (Union of Upper Silesia, ZG) was the most influential Silesian association. Its members held important local positions such as those of *voïvod* and of mayor and espoused a pro-Polish version of Silesian identity (Pędziwiatr, 2009). However, ZG, which had no concrete programme other than the revival of Silesian traditions, lost its importance by the end of the decade to the better-structured parallel Silesian organization, the Movement for the Autonomy of Silesia (RAŚ) (Majcherkiewicz, 2006: 264–268). RAŚ' activists seek to 'awaken' Silesians (phase B) and challenge the Polish national narrative while demanding regional autonomy similar to that accorded to the region in the interwar period (Pędziwiatr, 2009; Bieda, 2006: 10; Cybula and Majcherkiewicz, 2005: 150). Claims for territorial autonomy and for the recognition of Silesian nationality are associated however with "separatism" by the Polish state (Poland State Security Department, 2000).

From the beginning, RAŚ has behaved as a proto-party: in everyday activities it concentrates on culture and local problems, while, during electoral campaigns, it changes its discourse and uses its structures to promote a political programme (Wódz and Wódz, 2006: 68; Bałdys and Geisler, 2008: 106). The core of its programme is related to territorial autonomy. One of the pamphlets distributed in Katowice in 1997 says: "Upper Silesia is still treated as a colony [by Warsaw]. The rights of the people who should be hosts here are not respected ... In reaction to Warsaw's centralism and arrogance we demand autonomy" (in Wróblewski, 2006: 245). RAŚ, with 400 000 votes, elected two deputies in 1991, but the electoral system changed in 1993, introducing a 5% threshold that impeded further parliamentary success. Indeed, in 1993, according to Kijonka (2004: 39), RAŚ received 'only' 1.92% of votes in Upper Silesia. In 1997, RAŚ candidates appeared on the lists of Unia Polityki Realnej and RAŚ members ran for the Senate. None of them won any seats and the three candidates to the Senate together received 100 000 votes. The 2004 European elections were no better for the movement despite the candidacy of the RAŚ leader himself, Jerzy Gorzelik (Wróblewski, 2006; Bałdys and Geisler, 2008). According to Nijakowski (2004: 147), Gorzelik received 2360 votes, which represented only 0.3% of the total votes cast in the electoral district. Despite unsuccessful attempts in countrywide elections, RAŚ gained some representation at the local level in Śląskie. In the 2002 regional elections, with 4.35% of votes cast, no RAŚ candidate got into the Śląskie Parliament, but some were elected to municipal councils (Bałdys and Geisler, 2008: 107). In 2010, RAŚ' position significantly improved, as three RAŚ members, one of whom was Gorzelik with 14 345 votes, entered the Śląskie Parliament and formed the governing coalition with countrywide political parties Civic Platform (PO) and the Polish People's Party (PSL).

RAŚ' main objective is regional autonomy. It was only in 1996 that the idea of the 'Silesian nation' emerged from the Silesian Academic Association, linked to RAŚ. Consequently, the Union of People of Silesian *Nationality* was formed (ZLNŚ; Gorzelik, 2004: 16)—an association of the Silesian *national minority* ('mniejszosc narodowa') with the objective (Statut, part II.7-1) to activate and crystallize the Silesian *national consciousness* ('swiadomosc narodowa') (official ZLNS website). According to Gorzelik (2004: 27), in the context of RAŚ' political stagnation in the mid-1990s, the formation of ZLNŚ marks the movement's change in strategy. During the 1997 electoral campaign, activists from ZNLŚ displayed Silesian flags and slogans such as: "We are a nation and nobody can take that from us!" (Wróblewski, 2006: 243). ZNLŚ, however, is still not legally registered in the official registry of associations, foundations and other social and professional organizations. The initial registration in 1996 by the regional Katowice Court was successfully contested in court and, in subsequent decisions, other courts have refused to create a precedent which would point to the existence of a Silesian nation. The Union sent the case to the European Court of Human Rights, without success (Janicki, 2009; Kranz, 1998; Gerlich, 2002; Dembinska, 2008). A parallel organization, independent of RAŚ, the Association of Individuals of Silesian Nationality (SONŚ) was founded in early 2011 and registered in the Opole regional court in November but is now also being contested by the prosecutor. Whatever the final result, the conflict over these associations' registration has helped raise awareness of the cause. Gorzelik is explicit about this: "directing this affair on the legal track has guaranteed access to the main media ... There is no doubt that the [2002] census results are the effect of all this process. In 20th–21st centuries the time necessary to pass to the higher level of nation-building is significantly shorter" (quoted in Kijonka-Niezabitowska, 2009: 89).

In addition to the Polish political and legal arenas, Europe has been used to legitimize the Silesian national movement and territorial cause (Bałdys and Geisler, 2008: 110; Dembinska, 2012). RAŚ has adapted its discourse, claiming that Silesian autonomy corresponds to the Europe-wide decentralization process. The title of the main RAŚ journal refers to the 'Europe of 100 Flags', a concept used by the European alliance of regional political parties (DPPE-EFA), which RAŚ joined after the 2004 EU enlargement. Although not recognized as a distinct group by the Polish state, Silesians have gained a public voice and their demands are being legitimized through European institutions. RAŚ also uses its European network to offer seasonal jobs in the Basque country to unemployed miners from Silesia, for example (Bałdys and Geisler, 2008: 113). Such actions are a direct response to regional socio-economic problems and thus enhance RAŚ' image and legitimacy.

It is important to note that, given the ethnodemographic break-down in the region that results from twentieth century population forced and induced movements, RAŚ' strategy is to target all inhabitants of Silesia, not only the native population (Bałdys and Geisler 2008: 113). Their goal is to construct a regional identity to legitimize regional autonomy. It is consistent with Gorzelik's position on the subjective definition of nationality: the Silesian nation is to be formed by all those who identify as such. The

Silesian community is to be re-imagined but, as we shall see, it is re-imagined to fit the collective memories of the native population. Such an ambiguity in nation construction is not unusual: inclusive/civic nations are built around an ethnic core, civic/ethnic dichotomy is a question of degree (Smith, 1991; Kymlicka, 1995; Brubaker, 1999; Kuzio, 2002).

Activating Identity Attributes of Ethnogenesis and Language

Adopting a subjective definition of nationhood, the 2002 census results were presented by the Silesian organizations as the ultimate proof of the existence of the Silesian nation (Wróblewski, 2006: 240 and 247; Łodziński, 2008: 37). But their strategies had to adapt to a new context: the 2005 Law on National and Ethnic Minorities and the Regional Language, which provides 'objective' criteria for recognizing minorities and lists 14 groups, omitting Silesians. In order to get on that list and to legitimize the national movement in the eyes of the Polish state it was necessary to conform (Dembinska, 2008). Since having a 'distinct culture' and a 'distinct language' is one of the Law's criteria, efforts are being deployed to activate historical myths and to standardize the Silesian ethnolect. These efforts are to provide the needed 'proof' of groupness while negotiating with the Polish state. Returning to Hroch's nation-building phases, we could thus argue that the contemporary Silesian movement started with phase B and only seriously began phase A later and—apparently—instrumentally.

The formal requirement of a strongly distinct culture reinforces the development of the Silesian 'imagined community'. Silesian entrepreneurs present the group as a European collectivity and underline its distinctiveness from the Polish national community: Silesia

> was the Reich's second-largest industrial area when the remainder of partitioned Poland was still just fields ... a new model of man, of society [was born in Silesia] ... a certain work ethic, but also a certain understanding of political culture, of social responsibility ... so it has always been free of the absolutist traditions of the East [including Poland]. (K. Kutz, quoted in Białasiewicz, 2002: 123)

Scholars thus enquire into and disseminate the awareness of Silesian attributes, central processes of phase A. There is a great number of books now published on the region, among them Dariusz Jerczyński's (2003) *History of the Silesian Nation* referred to by Gorzelik on numerous occasions. This historiography, as with all national histories, presents the long life of its protagonist, the Silesian nation. According to Wróblewski (2006: 248–250; also Kurcz, 2008: 67–71), a number of historical myths serve to legitimize the present-day Silesian nation. According to the myth of descendancy, since the seventh century, Silesia has been inhabited by diverse Slavic tribes, all speaking a Slavic language—Silesian is thus a language and not a mere dialect. The population of Silesia was then characterized by multiple Slavo-germano-celtic origins. The author underlines the fact that Silesia converted to Christianity 103 years before Poland. The Silesian Golden Age was in the thirteenth century when two Silesian principalities were formed, one with its centre in Wroclaw, the other in Opole. These were the first Silesian political entities.

The myth of decline is associated with the Habsburgs and with the Austro-Prussian wars for Silesia. There are three victimization myths. First, the three Silesian insurrections after World War I that pitted inhabitants willing to join Germany against those willing to join Poland are interpreted as civil wars fomented by external actors. The second is the period of massive deportation to the USSR after the war and the third the experience of "Polish concentration camps for Silesians". The Silesians are presented as an oppressed nation, forcibly assimilated into neighbouring nations who occupied the Silesian national territory. The national liberalization myth accounts for the continuous Silesian aspiration for political representation, associated with Gajda (1849), Kożdoń (1909) and Sroka (1921), the latter advocating an independent state of Upper Silesia. Jerczyński (2003), the Silesian national ideologue and entrepreneur, concludes his *History of the Silesian Nation* by stating that, were it not for the oppressors, the Upper Silesian Republic would now be a well-developed medium-sized European state with five million inhabitants (see Kurcz, 2008: 72).

Silesian organizations' activities aim to disseminate this version of Silesian history, along with its culture, monuments and heroes. One of the strategies is to appropriate national symbols, such as great past figures (the 11 Nobel Prize winners from the region, for example) usually associated with Silesia's German origins (Wróblewski, 2006: 241–242). RAŚ organizes conferences, public gatherings and tours across Śląskie and Opolskie, notably during the 'Days of the Upper Silesian Heritage'. It has also initiated the digitalization of the Silesian press from the past, regardless of the language in which it was published (Bałdys and Geisler, 2008: 105).

Language constitutes another identity attribute activated by Silesian national entrepreneurs in their battle for recognition by the Polish state. In addition to its communicative functions, the Silesian ethnolect constitutes an important element of identification. According to the Polish linguist Bogusław Wyderka, Silesian had acquired this function by the second half of the nineteenth century when it began to be used to distinguish 'us' from 'them'. Independently of scientific opinions, which do not recognize Silesian as a language, this identification function persists and is part of the mythological Silesian consciousness (Wyderka, 2004: 199). The work of another linguist, Tomasz Kamusella, who argues that Silesian is a Creole language, has been eagerly used by the national movement to try to 'prove' that it does not constitute a mere dialect of the Polish language (Wyderka, 2004: 199).

Given the lack of a codified literate Silesian and the presumed existence of 13 variations of the ethnolect (for contrary opinions, see Semik, 2011 and Czesak, 2011), some effort at standardizing Silesian was in progress during the 1990s: the first Silesian–Polish dictionary was published in 1994, followed by two more in 1999 (Kamusella, 2011: 781). However, there has been a notable intensification of Silesian linguistic politics since the announcement of the Law on Minorities (Czesak, 2004; Kamusella, 2004a; Dembinska, 2008). One Silesian activist, Adam Rygjou, has claimed that Silesian will disappear if it does not receive state support and, in order to gain that support, according to linguist Jolanta Tambor, Silesians must proceed with linguistic standardization (Dembinska, 2012). There has been considerable effort to write and publish Silesian poetry and legends that, until recently, had been transmitted only orally. In 2005, books published by the Silesian *National* Publishing House owned by Andrzej Roczniok (the ZNLŚ leader) entered the mainstream Polish book market. In 2007, the Silesian language was attributed an ISO code by the Library of Congress, Washington, D.C., and in 2008 a Silesian Wikipedia emerged. In 2007, Roczniok started publishing the first-ever monthly periodical in Silesian (Kamusella, 2011: 781). The principles of the Silesian orthography were adopted in 2009. According to Kamusella (2011: 782 and 784), the Silesian language has acquired cultural and social capital, and its recognition would give it symbolic prestige and status. It would ensure the establishment of an 'ecological niche'. Phases A and B occur simultaneously.

Institutionalizing the Silesian Regional Language Category

An opportunity for recognizing the Silesian language unexpectedly emerged from the 2005 Law itself. Following the category of 'regional language group' created in the European Charter on Minority and Regional Languages (1995), the 2005 Polish law recognized the Kashub regional language group, Kashubian having been until then considered a mere dialect of Polish (Dembinka, 2012). The Silesian movement thus began exploring the possibility of re-opening the Law in order to add Silesian to this regional language category. Closely linked with RAŚ, a new organization, Pro Loquela Silesiana, was set up in 2007 in order to standardize the Silesian orthography, grammar and lexis. In 2008, together with RAŚ and ZG, it issued a petition to the members of the Polish Parliament from the region (Pędziwiatr, 2009). As a result, Lucjan Karasiewicz, Marek Plura and 21 other MPs proposed an amendment to the 2005 Law. The Parliamentary Committee on Minorities met three times—on 3 December 2008, 10 June 2010 and 27 July 2011—specifically to discuss the status of Silesian among deputies, government representatives, academic specialists and group representatives (Polish Parliament, 2008; 2010; 2011).

Following presentations by linguists and sociologists, the Committee agreed in 2008 that dialects may eventually develop into languages, but that this is a dynamic process involving codification as well as the use of the literary, standardized form by the population—a phase still limited in the Silesian case. Thus, efforts to codify the language were further intensified as of December 2008. The Committee met again with all the representatives in June 2010, including the Ministry of Interior Affairs and Administration (MSWiA). Given that the 2008 Committee's requirements were thought to have been fulfilled, the question was: 'What else do we need to do?' From the exchanges, it is quite clear that the Ministry's negative opinion was for political reasons rather than linguistics. Claims for territorial autonomy and 'Silesian nation' are still viewed as threatening Polish interests. The July 2011 session took place after the first parliamentary reading of the project amending the 2005 Law. The same arguments were repeated, and on both sides the work of linguists was cited. The Committee agreed to form a sub-committee to study the issue. This may mean that the project will not be adopted before the next elections—and thus it will have to start over again. An additional Committee meeting was scheduled for January 2012 in order to discuss the 2011 census results, but, since these were still unavailable, it was cancelled. Meantime, in March 2012, SONŚ, together with Kaszëbskô

Jednota—an association for people of 'Kashubian nationality'—published a petition demanding the recognition of these groups' as 'ethnic minorities', a level of recognition, between that of regional language group and national minority, the latter accorded to groups having a kin-state.

A Crystallized Silesian Nation? Identity of the Categorized

These political activities, together with the census results appear to achieve the institutionalization of the Silesian language and of the Silesian national category. Did Silesian nation-building enter Hroch's phase C? Sociological research shows that mass mobilization for the idea of the Silesian nation is rather limited. The explanation for this weakness resides in structural changes in the region as well as in transnational processes. Both these elements are transforming identity attributes and leading to the development of complementary 'occasional' identifications.

Structural Changes Transforming Silesianness: Attributes of Culture and Language

Silesia is the most industrialized Polish region. The post-communist economic re-structuring, involving liquidation of the mines and factories, put a huge burden on the inhabitants. The perception of Silesia as an 'internal colony' re-emerged (Nycz, 2010: 57; for a historical account of the region's marginalization, Szmeja, 2000). The dramatic structural and economic changes in Silesia may help explain declarations of 'Silesian nationality'. Some Silesians also believe that emphasizing the national dimension might help Silesia become a European region in a 'Europe of regions'. Given that the latter replacing a state-centered EU is considered unrealistic, these aspirations should be understood in terms of what Moore calls a 'region *in* Europe' within a 'Europe *for* regions', that is to be in the game by institutionalizing a regional voice in Brussels (Moore, 2008: 517–518 and 532—my italics; Nijakowski, 2006: 150–151; Kijonka-Niezabitowska, 2009: 104). According to sociological research conducted by Kurcz (2008) and Dolińska (2010), Silesian socio-cultural characteristics have been transformed with the modernization of the regional economy, the weakening of traditional Silesian workplaces, and the onset of transnational processes. Unemployment, post-1989 patterns of migration, and new mechanisms of diffusion of a common popular culture all play a role in social and identity transformations. The attributes of Silesianness, as activated by ethnic entrepreneurs, are negotiated and undermined (Kurcz, 2006: 361; 2008: 66; Szczepański, 2007). We are certainly witnessing an identity transformation process resulting from these socio-economic changes and the variety of opportunities Europeanization allows (Nijakowski, 2006: 154). What does 'Silesian nationality' mean for those who self-identified as such in the census? In 2008, Kurcz argued that the Silesian nation exists mainly in the ideology of the Silesian entrepreneurs. Phase C and the formation of sharp group boundaries are limited.

Rich sociological research, with extensive interviews, has been conducted in the region over the past six decades. All the authors agree that four ethnic attributes are associated with the Silesian culture—as observed by them and perceived by their respondents: the importance of family, religiosity, a work ethic and the Silesian ethnolect (Czech, 2006: ch. 2; Kurcz, 2008; Dolińska, 2009: 35; 2010: 76; Świątkiewicz-Mośny, 2010: 89; Buchowski and Chlewińska, 2012). These attributes are now activated by ethnopolitical organizations in order to underline Silesian specificity in opposition to Poles and to Germans. However, recent studies show a discrepancy between the traditional content of these attributes and their re-appropriation. Silesian families traditionally stick together. They meet regularly, organize extended family gatherings and maintain thick family social networks. In Kurcz's (2008: 76) recent analysis, most respondents agreed to attribute a social function to relations among family and neighbours: they help overcome difficulties, attain success, and contribute to the perception of security, belonging, recognition, and intimacy. However, respondents tend to acknowledge that family is losing these traditional functions because of a growing preoccupation with material goods, regional structural changes and the widespread use of electronic devices for professional communication and leisure.

The second distinctive characteristic of Silesianness is religiosity (see Czech, 2006: 63–70). Like ethnic Poles, Silesians are mostly Catholic, but, as research shows, they see their practice differently. They have their own symbolic places, such as pilgrimage sites (Saint Anna Mountain) and their own venerated saints, especially Saint Barbara, the patron of the miners. Typically, Silesians, unlike Poles, would own and use prayer books, whose use "grants a specific atmosphere to the mass" (Czech, 2006: 66). This tradition is traced back to the first publication of a prayer book by father Skowronek in the early 1900s, interestingly in Polish (*Droga do nieba*) and in German (*Weg zum Himmel*). "Poles are proud and happy when Pope John Paul II comes but then they do not follow [the] Pope's teachings on religious practice"—contrary to Silesians—said one of the respondents (Kurcz, 2008: 77). Silesians, unlike Poles, dissociate religion from the nation and from patriotism: "Silesians do not mix" these things, one respondent said. Still, Kurcz remarks a new phenomenon: migration, higher education, new workplaces, and foreign examples are all transforming attitudes towards faith and religious practices. Some respondents "fail to live up to Silesian standards of piety": they admit that they do not go to Church every Sunday and that they do not use the prayer book anymore (Kurcz, 2008: 78).

Third, the Silesian work *ethos* is another identity attribute that is brought up in sociological research. Because of their 'second class' status throughout history, Silesians were not owners but rather manual workers. Over time, a 'work cult' developed: a job, any job, has to be fulfilled with pleasure and passion, if not it would not be done well. Not only should one work well but each worker should also develop the ability to accomplish a variety of tasks, such as building a house or repairing a car. Industrial restructuring, unemployment, and work migration have transformed this ethos: people have less respect for work due to constant job uncertainty (Kurcz, 2008: 79). Kurcz concludes that, although Silesians do perceive themselves as distinct, globalization and the concomitant transformation processes are diminishing the importance of traditional Silesian values (Kurcz, 2008: 80). He remarks that protecting Silesian values and traditions is important for respondents but it is not expressed in terms of identification with a distinct nation and in opposition to ethnic Poles.

The Silesian ethnolect is a fourth important attribute of Silesianness, according to a study of Internet discussions by Świątkiewicz-Mośny (2010: 86). These exchanges are mostly in Silesian, but there is no one standardized form of the ethnolect: differences appear in spelling and in word choice in different dialectical/local forms of Silesian. On the one hand, new communication tools allow for the spread of the Silesian language community:

> the dynamically increasing use of Silesian in public discussion forums, websites, and news services may lead to the creation of a worldwide cyberspace Silesian 'speech community', at the very moment when actual Silesian speech communities in villages and old urban quarters gradually disappear, due to the rise in spatial and social mobility within postcommunist Poland and in the European Union more broadly. (Kamusella, 2011: 784)

On the other hand, despite efforts by Silesian activists to get the Silesian ethnolect recognized as a distinct language and marker of the Silesian nation, the Silesian vernacular is still considered by its speakers as most appropriate for speaking with family and neighbours (Kamusella, 2011: 784); a language of the heart, that has a limited public role. Among Silesian youth, the language of social communication is Polish, but, at home, a significant majority of them still use Silesian (70%). Indeed, young people learn Polish, and English or German as second language, in order to increase their career opportunities. As a consequence, the Silesian ethnolect has been gradually eliminated from the public sphere (Janicki, 2009: 17; Nijakowski, 2004). Research shows that fewer and fewer people use it, "young people increasingly avoid it, and above all, they mostly limit themselves to the Polish language outside the family" (Niedźwiedzki, 2011: 4). One of Niedźwiedzki's respondents says:

> Our grandchildren, one is 21, the other one is 16 years old, they are able to speak Silesian. Of course . . . But they can also speak very nice Polish. And they do so. We don't know when. When at home they speak Silesian.

Speaking Polish is easier: "The language has a larger vocabulary. Silesian limits the speaker. The Silesian dialect is limited . . . There are only a few words and that's all", affirms another respondent (Niedźwiedzki, 2011: 5). The Silesian ethnolect certainly lacks a complete repertoire of functions (Wyderka, 2004: 215). However, since it has an important identification role, respondents perceive these linguistic changes as a threat to the survival of the Silesian identity (Niedźwiedzki, 2011: 4). The ethnolinguistic organizations thus argue that the Silesian language should be recognized in order to ensure its survival. The Polish state responds that the Silesian ethnolect is already protected, as it is subject to the 1999 law on the preservation of regional cultural variations of Polishness. Although the survival of this 'language of the heart' seems important to self-identified Silesians, defining their ethno-regional community, it is not clear that they automatically espouse the idea of giving their ethnolect a legal 'language status' and the notion of a 'Silesian nation', characteristic of phase C.

Multiple, Fluctuating Identifications and Silesian National Consciousness

Census declarations indicate that Silesians do have a sense of group distinctiveness but it does not necessarily translate into a consciousness of nationhood. Silesia constitutes a sociological borderland that results in an 'indifference' to any national identification among the native population. Given the historic context as well as post-census opinion polls, Nijakowski argues that the rather vague and open census question brought people to interpret it in terms of their closest reference group, not national membership (Nijakowski, 2006: 149–150). This is also apparent in Niedźwiedzki's (2011: 10) interviews: "well, above all, [I am] a native Silesian. And when there was that census two or three years ago I said the same thing". Silesians constitute a classic borderland community that has an emotional attachment to the territory it inhabits. Due to frequent state changes, the only element of stability is the territory where people's grandparents were born (Nycz, 2010: 58) and where family graves are located (Kłoskowska, 2005: 247). Note that the emphasis placed on these territorially defined collective memories is somewhat at odds with the above-mentioned RAŚ strategy aimed at all present-day inhabitants of Silesia—a strategy that is essential to legitimizing regional autonomy given the post-1945 ethnic make-up of Silesia.

A significant proportion of Silesians considers themselves different from Poles and from Germans and identifies with the region instead (in Popieliński's (2008: 129) study, 28.4% of young respondents in Upper Silesia did so). Dolińska's (2010) study demonstrates that the genealogical-emotional aspects, that is, being born on the territory where one's ancestors were born, constitute the decisive motivation for declaring oneself of Silesian nationality. Identifying themselves as members of a Silesian nationality in the census does not, however, mean that the respondents believe Silesia is a separate nation. One of the reasons, Niedźwiedzki (2011: 10) finds, is a belief that Silesianness does not contradict identification with the Polish nation:

> I'm proud that I am Silesian. I am proud, because I say that I was born here and I live here. If for example I was born in Warsaw, I would be proud that I am a Varsovian, a Pole. And here I am a Pole but of Silesian origin.

The lack of 'coherence' in declaring one's nationality, its changing character in an individual's lifetime, is typical of borderland communities. In these contexts the phenomenon of loyalty conversion—as sociologists call it—is not unusual (Kłoskowska, 1995; Nycz, 2010: 57). Borderland peoples do not like to choose between nations and rather prefer to identify with their immediate region (Szczepański, 2004; Wódz, 2007). They are patriots of their own small homeland, their "private homeland" (Ossowski, 1967). Silesians have a very strong regional attachment and a weakly developed ideological attachment (Popieliński, 2008: 128). For centuries, the choice between national identities depended on the relative attractiveness of different political options. The result of these processes is the characteristic "national indifference and instability" (Nycz, 2010: 57). Studying the German minority in Silesia, Popieliński remarks that, in the early 1990s, for a variety of reasons (passport, migration, job), many people entered German minority associations and considered themselves German. After a few years, however—disappointed with Germany and with Germans when travelling for jobs, it may be argued—many preferred to identify as Silesian. Some respondents also showed uneasiness when choosing between national categories and preferred to identify as students or human beings (Popieliński, 2008: 128, 130; 2011: 41, 197). This national diffusion or distraction, says Nycz (2010:

57), is typical of individuals belonging to two or more social and cultural worlds. Popieliński remarks that, if we do not see borderland identities in these terms, we cannot explain why, in the same family, individuals identify with different communities (Popieliński, 2008: 128 and 2011: 41). Such conceptions of identity are not easily reflected in official numbers provided by census data. This complexity is not exposed by Silesian ethnic entrepreneurs either, as the numbers provide a good tool for legitimizing their claims.

Silesians have both Polish and German origins and traditions (Szmeja, 1998: 60). Depending on their own personal experiences, each person decides how to identify him or herself, as Polish or German or Silesian or any dual identification. Duality is typical: when praying in Church, Silesians often use Silesian or German (older generation only), but, when they talk about John Paul II, they refer to him as "our Pope" (Kłoskowska, 2005: 246). Identifications here are multidimensional; they are a matter of "scaling" (Ossowski, 1967; Kłoskowska, 2005: 235). Not only can they be put on a spectrum: "Pole, Pole–Silesian, Silesian–Pole, Silesian, Silesian–German, German–Silesian, German", but each of these identifications changes its meaning over time (Bartoszek, 2009: 115–117; Dolińska, 2010: 79, 81; Świątkiewicz-Mośny, 2010: 86). Moreover, 7% of Popieliński's (2008: 131) respondents identified themselves as European. Traditional identity attributes are giving way to more multicultural and European attributes, especially among the young population (Kłoskowska, 2005: 247; Nycz, 2010: 70; Niedźwiedzki, 2011: 20). This does not mean that the Silesian identification is vanishing, rather that it is taking on different meanings while interacting with different cultures. As a result, its importance for social relations is decreasing. Researchers observe that young respondents self-identify at once as Polish, Silesian, European and German. Each identification has a distinct function. In other words, each takes precedence at a different time (Kłoskowska, 2005: 253; Kijonka-Niezabitowska, 2009: 85). Research among secondary school students in Silesia indicates clearly that teenagers coming from Silesian families do identify as such, but, at the same time, they negotiate this identity in a dynamic process of interactions within peer networks (Bartoszek, 2009: 111). Identity does not reproduce itself in a direct and linear fashion. Teenage culture and exchanges 'neutralize' individuals' links to their historic-symbolic environment and limit their ethno-regional family traditions, forming a transformed multidimensional post-modern identity (Bartoszek, 2009: 118). The youngest generation makes international rather than historic comparisons (Kłoskowska, 2005: 253). However, these identity transformations do not imply acculturation or assimilation.

As mentioned in the first section of this article, national self-identification is 'occasional' and reinforced in some specific social situations. The census is one such situation (Dolińska, 2010: 73). The Silesian entrepreneurs have not managed to massively convert Silesians to the idea that their identity is national (Wróblewski, 2006: 252) and thus to make progress from phases A and B to C. This is confirmed by Dolińska (2010): since there was no way to distinguish between ethnic and national categories in the 2002 census, Silesians chose the only category enabling them to declare group distinctiveness. Most of them, however, would rather talk of regional identity or ethnicity, but, as one respondent said: as a "nation, some kind of state or so. Let's not exaggerate" (Dolińska, 2010: 79). Kijonka-Niezabitowska (2009: 105) remarks that only RAŚ' members and its sympathizers indicate that their 2002 census declaration corresponded to their real feeling of belonging to the Silesian *nation*. Most respondents would like to be 'officially Silesian' but in what exact category is another question, one that Silesians do not like to be asked (Dolińska, 2010: 82). It is worth noting that a great number of Silesians are unable to identify their ethnic leaders or point to the organizations working for Silesians (Niedźwiedzki, 2011: 12). Interpreting the 2011 census results, Zygmunt Woźniczka, an expert from the University of Silesia, contends that the increase in the number of self-identified Silesians is a result of economic difficulties and a reaction to the years of central state failure to appreciate the region's inhabitants. He adds that, as soon as this situation is reversed or people have the opportunity to realize that Silesian autonomy cannot improve their lives, we will witness a significant decline in Silesian national identification (Kasprzyk, 2012).

Conclusion

The objective of this article was twofold: to explore the development and mobilization strategies of the Silesian ethnolinguistic movement in its quest for recognition and institutionalization of the Silesian national category; and to determine whether the growing numbers of mobilized Silesians correspond to the formation of a mass national consciousness which would constitute Hroch's phase C. Silesian organizations used standard nation-building techniques. They took advantage of the opening of the Polish state in order to put their claims for autonomy and for cultural recognition into the public sphere. They formed proto-party socio-cultural associations, participating in countrywide and regional elections. They managed subsequently to legitimize their claims through the European political system. By the mid-1990s, running out of steam, the idea of institutionalizing a *national* identity category emerged as a possible strategy to revitalize the movement, and a legal battle to register ZNLŚ begun, providing visibility to the cause. It was with the adoption of the 2005 Law and its criteria for group recognition that the process of nation-building, as such, took off. Ethnic entrepreneurs had to abandon the subjective definition of the nation, as they had to adapt to the objective definition used by the Polish state. The existence of a distinct culture and language had to be scientifically 'proven'. The movement increased its efforts to re-imagine Silesian historiography as well as to standardize the Silesian ethnolect. Thus, the activation of ethnic attributes was a response to the state and a requirement for the movement's future relations with Polish state representatives, rather than a policy directed solely to the categorized. The nation-building process was the reverse of Hroch's model: phase B preceded and then occurred simultaneously with phase A.

The Silesian national movement is having considerable success in institutionalizing the regional language and national identity categories. However, this article shows that it still lacks groupness, in Brubaker's terms. Although the ethnolinguistic group consciousness, associated with a 'private homeland' territory, is strong, the political-national consciousness of Silesianness is weak. It is an "identity in the heart" and a "language of heart", which contribute to a sense of otherness (Niedźwiedzki, 2011: 23). Silesian ethnic attributes are transformed due to a changing socio-economic context, but the efforts by ethnic entrepreneurs to transform Silesians into a full-blown nation are minimized by countervailing phenomena: transnationalism and modernization. Not only do Silesians identify more and more with the Polish nation, they also acquire a complementary European identification. Their identity is multidimensional and fluctuating (Kłoskowska, 1995; Hutchinson, 2000). Each identification of which this borderland identity is composed—be it Silesian, Polish, German or European—is 'occasional' because each has a different function. Consequently, depending on the context, the Silesian national category may appeal to different numbers of individuals.

More research should be conducted, but, just as the Silesian movement is taking advantage of structural openings, one can assume that the proliferation of ethnolinguistic mobilizations is strongly related to transnational processes. These same processes, paradoxically, limit the movements' ability to cross into phase C: the formation of a mass nation. Present-day socio-cultural dynamics make it difficult to fix stable self-identifications because boundaries between 'us' and 'them' tend to be blurred and to be transformed continuously as a result of accelerated interactions with the external world. This may have implications for Hroch's A–B–C model.

Acknowledgement

I would like to thank Katarzyna Karnaszewska for her excellent research. This article would not have been possible without her. I am also grateful to Alistair Cole and Jean-Baptiste Harguindéguy as well as to the anonymous reviewer for their very helpful comments that helped me to refine my argument. I also wish to thank Eric Guntermann for his excellent editing job.

References

Bałdys, P. and Geisler, R. (2008), 'Śląski neotrybalizm, in A. Sakson (ed.), *Ślazacy, Kaszubi, Mazurzy i Warmiacy*. Poznan: Instytut zachodni.

Bartoszek, A. (2009), Kapitał kulturowy a identyfikacje narodowo-etniczne młodych ślaząków, *Studia socjologiczne*, Vol.4, No.195, pp.111–128.

Białasiewicz, L. (2002), Upper Silesia, in J. Batt and K. Wolczuk (eds), *Region, State and Identity in Central and Eastern Europe*. London: Frank Cass.

Bieda, M. (2006), Naród czy polityczna gra? Conference paper, Department of Sociology, University of Bielsko-Biała. Available at http://www.socjologia.ath.bielsko.pl/prace/mbieda_slask.pdf (accessed 25 March 2012).

Brubaker, R. (1999), The Manichean Myth: Rethinking the Distinction Between 'Civic' and 'Ethnic' Nationalism, in H. Kriesi *et al.* (eds), *Nation and National Identity*, pp.55–73. Zurich: Variag Ruegger.

Brubaker, R. (2006), *Ethnicity Without Groups*. Cambridge: Harvard University Press.

Buchowski, M. and Chlewińska, K. (2012), Do Silesians Exist and can Silesia be Autonomous?, National Case Studies of Challenges to Tolerance in Political Life, Florence: European University Institute, Robert Schuman Centre for Advanced Studies.

Ciagwa, J. (1988), *Autonomia Slaska (1922–39)*. Katowice: Muzeum Slaskie.

Cybula, A. and Majcherkiewicz, T. (2005), Wielokulturowość regionu Środkowoeuropejskiego, *Sprawy narowodościowe*, Vol.26, pp.135–156.

Czech, H. (2006), *Ethos wsi śląskiej*. Warsaw: Trio.

Czesak, A. (2004), Ślązacy w poszukiwaniu języka, *Przegląd polonijny*, Vol.30, No.3, pp.105–112.

Czesak, A. (2011), 'Nowy' język śląski i legenda o 13 gwarach, *Danga*. Available at www.danga.pl/?p=766 (accessed 25 March 2012).

Dembinska, M. (2008), Adapting To Changing Contexts of Choice, *Canadian Journal of Political Science*, Vol.41, No.4, pp.915–934.

Dembinska, M. (2012), (Re)Framing Identity Claims, *Nations and Nationalism*, Vol.18, No.3, pp.417–438.

Dolińska, K. (2009), *Potoczny i ideologiczny poziom doświadczania śląskości*. Wrocław: Wydawnictwo Uniwersytetu Wrocławskiego.

Dolińska, K. (2010), Kryteria narodowej autoidentyfikacji Ślazaków, in R. Szwed, L. Dyczewski and J. Szulich-Kałuża (eds), *Odmiany tożsamości 3*. Lublin: Wydawnictwo KUL.

Gerlich, M. G. (1994), Śląska krzywda, *Etnografia polska*, Vol.38, Nos.1–2, pp.5–21.

Gerlich, M. G. (2002), Powoływanie narodu śląskiego, *Etnografia Polska*, Vol.46, Nos.1–2, pp.29–49.

Gorzelik, J. (2004), Ruch śląski, in L.N. Nijakowski (ed.), *Nadciągają Ślązacy*. Warsaw: SCHOLAR.

Hale, H. (2004), Explaining Ethnicity, *Comparative Political Studies*, Vol.37, No.4, pp.458–482.

Hroch, M. (1993), From National Movement to the Fully-formed Nation, *New Left Review*, Vol.a, No.198, pp.3–20.

Hutchinson, J. (2000), Ethnicity and Modern Nations, *Ethnic and Racial Studies*, Vol.23, No.4, pp.651–669.

Janicki, W. (2009), Minority Recognition in Nation-states, in T. Drobik and M. Sumberova (eds), *Chapters of Modern Human Geographical Thought*. Cambridge: Cambridge Scholar Publishing.

Jerczyński, D. (2003), *History of the Silesian Nation*. Gorny Slask: Narodowa Oficyna Wydawnicza.

Kamusella, T. (1994), Musisz być Niemcem, albo Polakiem, *Sprawy narodowościowe*, Nos.14/15, pp.113–123.

Kamusella, T. (1999), *The Dynamics of the Policies of Ethnic Cleansing in Silesia in the 19th and 20th Centuries*, Budapest: Open Society Institute, Electronic Publishing Program.

Kamusella, T. (2002), Nation-Building and the Linguistic Situation in Upper Silesia, *European Review of History: Revue europeenne d'histoire*, Vol.9, No.1, pp.37–62.

Kamusella, T. (2004a), Standardyzacja języka górnośląskiego, *Sprawy narodowościowe*, Vol.24–25, pp.113–131.

Kamusella, T. (2004b), The Szlonzokian Ethnolect in the Context of German and Polish Nationalisms, *Studies in Ethnicity and Nationalism*, Vol.4, No.1, pp.19–38.

Kamusella, T. (2011), Silesian in the Nineteenth and Twentieth Centuries, *Nationalities Papers*, Vol.39, No.5, pp.769–789.

Kasprzyk, M. (2012), Wyniki spisu, *Dziennik Zachodni*, 22 March 2012.

Kijonka, T. (2004), Po siedmiu latach kampanii, in L.N. Nijakowski (ed.), *Nadciągają Ślązacy*. Warsaw: SCHOLAR.

Kijonka-Niezabitowska, J. (2009), Z problemów narodowości i tożsamosci śląskiej, *Studia socjologiczne*, Vol.4, No.195, pp.85–110.

Kłoskowska, A. (1995), Otwarte i zamkniete postawy narodowe w sytuacji pogranicza, *Kultura i Spoleczenstwo*, No. 3.

Kłoskowska, A. (2005), *Kultury narodowe u korzeni*. Warsaw: Wydawnictwo naukowe PWN.

Kochanowski, J. (2001), Gathering Poles into Poland, in P. Ther (ed.), *Redrawing Nations*. New York: Rowman & Littlefield.

Kranz, J. (1998), A National Minority of Silesians?, *The Polish Quarterly of International Affairs*, Vol.7, No.4, pp.61–76.

Kurcz, Z. (2006), Postulowany naród śląski i śląska ideologia narodowa, in E. Michalik and H. Chałupczak (eds), *Mniejszości narodowe i etniczne w procesach transformacji oraz integracji*. Lublin: Wydawnictwo Uniwersytetu Marii Curie-Sklodowskiej.

Kurcz, Z. (2008), Naród śląski w świetle ideologii przodowników i w świadomości uczestników wyobrażonej wspólnoty, in A. Sakson (ed.), *Ślązacy, Kaszubi, Mazurzy i Warmiacy*. Poznań: Instytut zachodni.

Kurczewski, J. (2006), A Borderland in Midst of the Country, in J. Kurczewska (ed.), *Polish Borders and Borderlands in the Making*. Warsaw: IFiS.

Kuzio, T. (2002), The Myth of the Civic State: A Critical Survey of Hans Kohn's Framework for Understanding Nationalism, *Ethnic and Racial Studies*, Vol.25, No.1, pp.20–39.

Kymlicka, W. (1995), Misunderstanding Nationalism, *Dissent*, Winter, pp.130–135.

Linek, B. (2001), 'De-Germanization' and 'Re-Polonization' in Upper Silesia, in P. Ther and A. Siljak (eds), *Redrawing Nations*. Lanham, MD: Rowman and Littlefield.

Lodzinski, S. (2008), Instytucje i tozsamosc etniczna, in A. Sakson (ed.), *Slazacy, Kaszubi, Mazurzy i Warmiacy*. Poznan: Instytut Zachodni.

Máiz, R. and Requejo, F. (eds) (2005), *Democracy, Nationalism and Multiculturalism*. London: Frank Cass.

Majcherkiewicz, T. (2006), Gorny Slask – Opinie regionalnych elit administracyjnych, in Z. Leszkowicz-Baczyńska (ed.), *Transgranicznosc w perspektywie socjologicznej*. Zielona Gora: Lubuskie Towarzystwo Naukowe.

Majewicz, A. (1989), *Języki świata i ich klasyfikowanie*. Warsaw: PWN.

May, S., Modood, T. and Squires, J. (eds) (2004), *Ethnicity, Nationalism and Minority Rights*. Cambridge: Cambridge University Press.

Moore, C. (2008), A Europe of the Regions vs. the Regions in Europe, *Regional and Federal Studies*, Vol.18, No.5, pp.517–535.

Mucha, J. L. (1992), Democratization and Cultural Minorities, *East European Quarterly*, Vol.25, No.4, pp.463–482.

Mucha, J. L. (1997), Getting Out of the Closet, *East European Quarterly*, Vol.31, No.3, pp.299–309.

Niedźwiedzki, D. (2011), Regional, Ethnic, European?, *Reconstituting Democracy in Europe*. Oslo: University of OsloRECON Online Working Paper 2011/33. Available at www.reconproject.eu/projectweb/portalproject/RECONWorkingPapers.html (accessed 25 March 2012).

Nijakowski, L. M. (2004), O procesach narodowotwórczych na Śląsku, in L.N. Nijakowski (ed.), *Nadciagaja Slazacy*. Warsaw: SCHOLAR.

Nijakowski, L. M. (2006), Status grup etnicznych oraz mniejszości narodowych i etnicznych w Polsce, in L. Adamczuk and S. Łodziński (eds), *Mniejszości narodowe w Polsce w świetle Narodowego Spisu Powszechnego z 2002 roku*. Warsaw: SCHOLAR.

Nycz, E. (2010), Polak-Ślązak-Niemiec, in R. Szwed, L. Dyczewski and J. Szulich-Kałuża (eds), *Odmiany tożsamości 3*. Lublin: KUL.

Ossowski, S. (1967), Analiza socjologiczna pojęcia ojczyzna, in *Dzieła: Z zagadnień psychologii społecznej*. Warszawa.

Pędziwiatr, K. (2009), Silesian Autonomist Movement in Poland. Research project *L'Europe rebelle*, Tischner European University and Université Paris-Est. Available at www.wse.krakow.pl/pl/download/file/f,585 (accessed 25 March 2012).

Poland, State Security Department (2000), *Raport dotyczący zagrożeń dla bezpieczeństwa państwa*. Available at www.videofact.com/mark/uop/uop1.html (accessed 25 March 2012).

Polish Parliement (2008, 2010, 2011), Commission on Minorities, minutes, No. 30, 1588/VI kad., (3.12.2008); No.61, 3826/VI kad. (10.06.2010); No.5396/VI kad. (27.07.2011). Available at http://orka.sejm.gov.pl/Biuletyn.nsf (accessed 25 March 2012).

Popieliński, P. (2008), Młodzi ślązacy między niemickościa a polskościa, in A. Sakson (ed.), *Ślązacy, Kaszubi, Mazurzy i Warmiacy*. Poznań: Instytut zachodni.

Popielinski, P. (2011), *Mlodziez mniejszosci niemieckiej na Gornym Slasku po 1989 roku*. Warsaw: Instytut Studiow Politycznych PAN.

Ruszczewski, J. (1995), Etniczność a konflikty społeczne na Śląsku Opolskim, *Przegląd polonijny*, Vol.21, No.1, pp.101–113.

Sekuła, E. A. (2010), Kultury pamięci Górnoślązaków, in S. Kapralski (ed.), *Pamięć, przestrzeń, tożsamość*. Warsaw: SCHOLAR.

Semik, T. (2011), Nasza godka to nie język, *Dziennik Zachodni*, 18 February 2011.

Simonides, D. (2004), Śląskie kłopoty z tożsamością, in L.M. Nijakowski (ed.), *Nadciagaja Ślązacy*. Warsaw: SCHOLAR.

Skomorowska, A. (2012), Mniej Niemców, więcej Ślązaków, *Radio Opole*, 22 March 2012.

Smith, A. D. (1991), *National Identity*. London: Penguin.

Stroschein, S. (2011), Microdynamics of Bilateral Ethnic Mobilization, *Ethnopolitics*, Vol.10, No.1, pp.1–34.

Suchocka, R. (2006), Tożsamość i obywatelstwo w warunkach pogranicza, in Z. Leszkowicz-Baczyńska (ed.), *Transgraniczność w perspektywie socjologicznej*. Zielona Gora: Lubuskie Towarzystwo Naukowe.

Świątkiewicz, W. (2005), Spory o symbole, in L. Dyczewicz (ed.), *Kultura grup mniejszosciowych i marginalnych*. Lublin: KUL.

Świątkiewicz-Mośny, M. (2010), Ślązacy na *Naszej klasie*, in R. Szwed, L. Dyczewski and J. Szulich- Kałuża (eds), *Odmiany tożsamości 3*. Lublin: KUL.

Szczepański, M. (1997), Region pogranicza i pogranicza w regionie, *Gazeta uniwersytecka Uniwersytetu Śląskiego*. Available at http://gu.us.edu.pl/node/241781 (accessed 7 December 2012).

Szczepański, M. (2004), Regionalizm górnośląski, in L.N. Nijakowski (ed.), *Nadciągają Ślązacy*. Warsaw: SCHOLAR.

Szczepański, M. (2007), Od Szramka do społeczeństw sieciowych, in P. Bałdys and K. Piątek (eds), *Regiony pogranicza w dobie integracji europejskiej*. Bielsko-Biała.

Szmeja, M. (1998), Historyczne i społeczne uwarunkowania powstawania mniejszości niemieckiej i narodu śląskiego, *Studia socjologiczne*, Vol.4, No.151, pp.39–65.

Szmeja, M. (2000), *Niemcy? Polacy? Ślązacy!*. Kraków: Kraków.

Szmeja, M. (2002), Identyfikacja narodowa Ślązaków na Opolszczyźnie, *Przegląd polonijny*, Vol.28, No.2, pp.43–53.

Vural, Y. and Rustemli, A. (2006), Identity Fluctuations in the Turkish Cypriot Community, *Mediterranean Politics*, Vol.11, No.3, pp.329–348.

Wilson, T. M. and Donnan, H. (eds) (1998), *Border Identities*. Cambridge: Cambridge University Press.

Wódz, K. (2007), Silesian Identity in a Region of the Polish State, in D. M. Smith and E. Wistrich (eds), *Regional Identity and Diversity in Europe*. London: Federal Trust for Education and Research.

Wódz, K. and Wódz, J. (2006), *Dimensions of Silesian Identity*. Katowice: Wydawnictwo Uniwersytetu Śląskiego.

Wróblewski, P. (2006), Typy legitymacji narodowości śląskiej a Narodowy Spis Powszechny z 2002 roku, in L. Adamczuk and S. Łodziński (eds), *Mniejszości narodowe w Polsce w świetle Narodowego Spisu Powszechnego z 2002 roku*. Warsaw: SCHOLAR.

Wyderka, B. (2004), Język, dialekt czy kreol? in L.N. Nijakowski (ed.), *Nadciągają Ślązacy*. Warsaw: SCHOLAR.

Young, I. M. (2002), Self-Determination and Global Democracy, in B. Helmbrecht, J. Gebhardt and K. Losch K (eds), *Multiculturalism in Contemporary Societies*. Erlangen, Germany: Universitatsbund Erlangen.

Doing As They Are Told? Subregional Language Policies in the Basque Country, Catalonia and Wales

PATRICK CARLIN

School of Welsh, Cardiff University, Cardiff UK

ABSTRACT This article analyses efforts by subregional government to plan for and implement language policy (LP). It aims to show that this governance level is key to a more nuanced understanding of the locations within which language policies are created, brought to fruition and evaluated. With this in mind, data from six subregional authorities in the Autonomous Community of the Basque Country, the Autonomous Community of Catalonia and Wales are employed. Additionally, from the particularity of each region and subregional authority, these data are applied more generally to analyse party political support for LP activity as well as LP interaction across governance tiers. This paper discusses the extent to which regional governments' legislative and fiscal support (or relative lack of support) for overall LP objectives influences, restricts or otherwise engages subregional government LP activity. Understanding the relationship between the first two objectives will help to link local empirical data with the third objective—that of beginning to unravel the role that non-statewide nationalist and regional branches of statewide political parties play as LP facilitators at both subregional and regional level. Party activity in LP is subsequently interpreted as a measure through which to emphasize the values of (often overlapping) identity and solidarity patterns.

Introduction

The development of regional language policy (LP) and planning by both non-statewide parties and regional branches of statewide parties have been the subject of only a few, albeit in-depth, area study analyses (for example, Argelaguet, 1998; 2007). More specifically, the outworking of LP within intergovernmental interactions and transactions has been examined from within different disciplines and focused overwhelmingly at the regional level (Wright, 2004; Agirreazkuenaga, 2005: 19; Williams, C. 2007: 302). However, although there have been contributions dealing with the relations between regional and subregional governance in general (Cole, 2006;

Agranoff, 2010), fuller description and analysis of how subregional LP impacts upon, and is impacted by, interactions within the totality of political and institutional regional systems are lacking.

This article acknowledges that significant policy responsibilities rest at the subregional level and that if the outworkings of LP within both territorial, jurisdictional and functional understandings of multi-level governance are to be fully realized, then more scrutiny should be devoted to the subregional level. Whilst a more critical sub-literature of LP has acknowledged human agency and a range of identitarian orientations and political motivations linked to language policy (Williams and Morris, 2000; Lo Bianco, 2004), subregional LP and its relationship to such orientations and motivations remains unproblematized and thus under-analysed.

Political parties are one of the main vehicles for a continuing democratic will as expressed by citizens (De Winter and Türsan, 1998), and one of the roles played is that of "ethnic political entrepreneurs" in a process of (re)construction of the regionalist "imagined community" and its subsequent claims for changing the existing centre/periphery power arrangements (Hepburn, 2009: 477). One of these claims lies in the practical and discursive use of the autochthonous language(s) historically connected to a given linguistic community.

This article focuses on actions by political parties engaged in sub-state territorial empowerment which either supports subregional LP or develops more guarded approaches to it, often due to opposing streams within the same party. Following an analysis of subregional LP activity in the three regions,[1] these linguistic interventions, understood as cultural markers for those political parties promoting the autochthonous language, will be contextualized within the regional political and institutional system. This paper concludes that further analysis is needed on the degree to which the politicization and mobilization of language claims by political parties occupying a range of territory and class cleavages become integrated into complex and changing multi-level constellations of power.

Internal LP Activity

Attempts to intervene in, and influence linguistic practices within subregional government, are readily visible in internal administration, as these are closest to human and budgetary capacities. The six case studies[2] (see Figures 1–4) exemplify that the most transparent way to implement language policy within internal subregional administration is via permissive regional or state legislation. Such legislation legitimizes subregional government intervention in the language practices of its officers and—to a lesser extent—elected members, as well as in the linguistic choices this governance level offers citizens. However, subregional government willingness to engage in this activity would be all the more evident were it not supported through regional language legislation. In this article, three LP orientations by subregional government are discerned, specifically in relation to subregional response to the existence or otherwise of regional language legislation. These are pre-emptive LP, adherent LP and reluctant LP. As will be exemplified, LP orientations within any given subregional government can change when variations occur in the regional structure or party base.

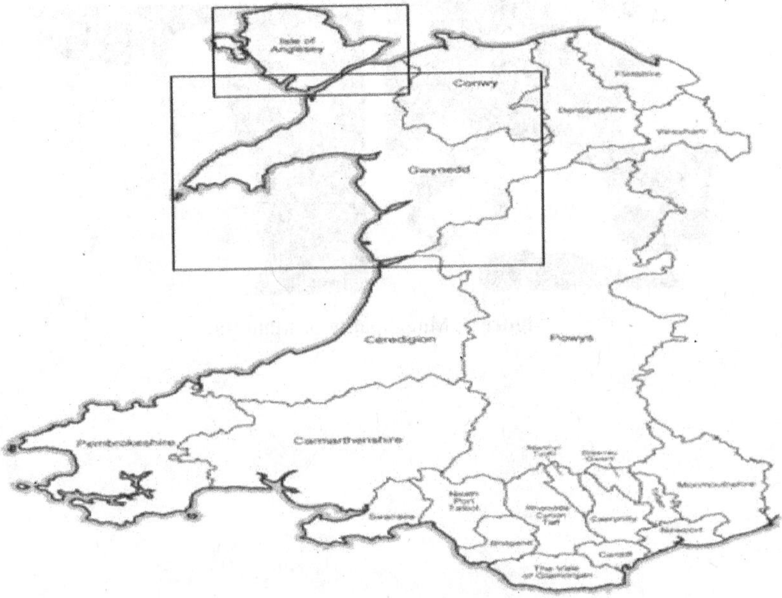

Figure 1. Gwynedd Council and Isle of Anglesey County Council.

Pre-emptive LP

The most striking cases of subregional LP are those cases whereby language policies were introduced irrespective of, and *before*, regional language legislation. In this category are Santa Coloma de Gramenet (SCG) between 1979 and 1991 and Gwynedd County Council between 1974 and 1993.[3]

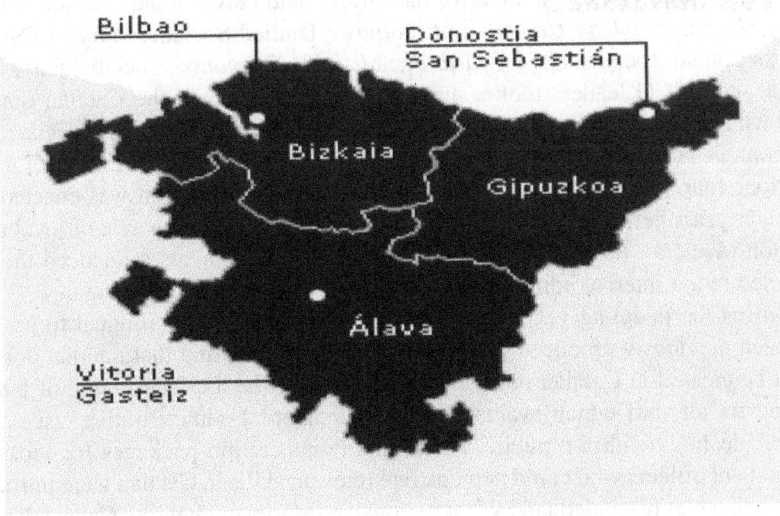

Figure 2. Gipuzkoa Provincial Council and Bizkaia Provincial Council.

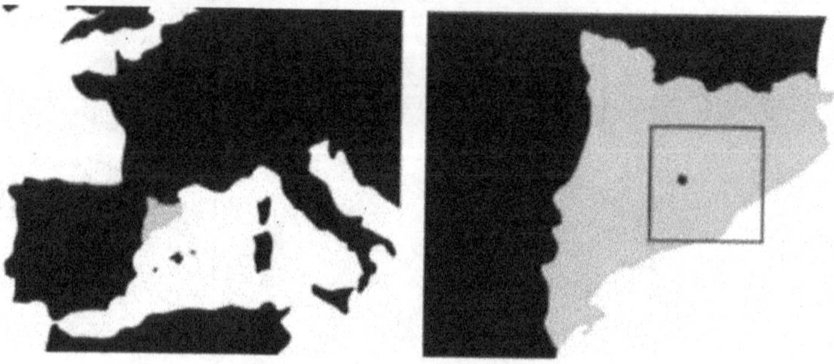

Figure 3. Municipality of Manresa.

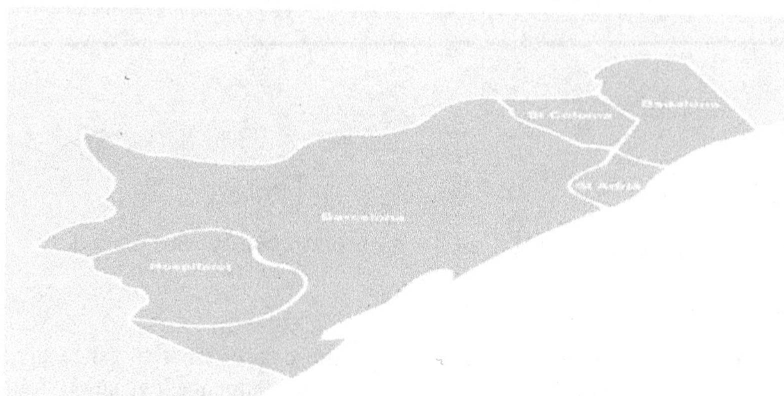

Figure 4. Municipality of Santa Coloma de Gramenet.

In 1979, with control of the town hall firmly held between the communists of the PSUC (*Partit Socialista Unificat de Catalunya*, Unified Socialist Party of Catalonia) and the Catalan socialists PSC (*Partit Socialista de Catalunya*, Socialist Party of Catalonia), core SCG leaders took a maximum interpretation of the Catalan Statute of 1979 which affirmed Catalan as the autochthonous language (*llengua pròpia*) for the autonomous community. Interview material shows that the cabinet of SCG took LP decisions four years before specific regional language legislation was enacted and a full eight years before the existence of regional legislation in the area of local administration (*Noticias Jurídicas*, 2012). These regional enactments influenced the status accorded to the internal administrative oral and written use of the language.

During the fledgling years of democracy, SCG introduced bilingual forms which had been previously produced in Spanish only whilst ensuring that internal documentation be created in Catalan only. This led in turn to the local designing of language skilling for all staff which evaluated both their internal administrative tasks as well as their dealings with the public. Additional remuneration packages for those local government officers who could demonstrate relevant skills in Catalan were introduced, but this step was rescinded later when regional legislation addressing Catalan language skills was deployed. As some of these internal developments were lacking in formal institutional support at the regional level, the SCG cabinet was unsure of the wisdom of officially recording many of these activities, specifically because the town hall might have been open to litigation through lack of legislative support:

> We never *took* that decision. That is, that particular decision was *voiced*, it was never minuted because if we had decided to go down that route, it would have complicated the myriad ways of interpreting it and, without a doubt, it would have ended up in litigation. If we had followed a route whereby we recommended a policy on the promotion of Catalan and then published it, we could have entered dangerous waters. (Interview with senior elected member, SCG)[4]

In the case of Gwynedd Council, the council's language policy, which began with the setting up of the council in 1974, received a greater degree of legislative legitimation in the form of the Welsh Language Act (WLA) enacted at Westminster almost 20 years later. The change-over period of local government reorganization in 1973–74 was, however, a political opportunity not to be missed. The shadow council created a tier of senior officers who could work in both languages and, in 1975, deputy senior officers were requested to be able to comply with the same requirement (Shadow Gwynedd County Council, 1973a). A Bilingual Sub-committee was created which was to wield substantial influence over public bodies not only across North Wales but nationally as well. In its early years, it focused on ensuring bilingual services for the public and developing language courses for officers. As regards the use of the language by elected members, the Sub-committee's aim was to establish the principle that Welsh should be made the language of the plenary sessions and sub-committees and, in this vein, a Translation Unit was set up to facilitate and extend the use of simultaneous translation.

In keeping with the uncertainty shown at SCG, Gwynedd harboured substantial doubts about its ability to push the policy forward due to indirect lines of communication with the Welsh Office in Cardiff and a legal regime unable to support its activity (Shadow Gwynedd County Council, 1973b; Thomas, 1997: 334). From 1964–99, the Welsh Office oversaw the growth of administrative devolution in Wales. This uncertainty would lead to a number of restrictions on the internal language policy, for example the unwillingness to usher in a requirement of Welsh for all officers and the lack of budgetary details concerning the rolling out and maintenance of the policy. Indeed, in 1985, the Council was involved in a legal dispute with both labour unions and the Commission for Racial Equality on this requirement (McLeod, 1998). Internal language policy was aversely affected by the publicity generated around this case (interview with senior officer, Gwynedd Council) and it was not until enactment of the WLA in 1993 and further local government reorganization in 1996 that Gwynedd designated Welsh as the administrative internal written and oral language, thus becoming the first county council tier of government within the United Kingdom to designate a non-statewide language the working language of internal administration.

Adherent LP

It is now time to turn to LP activities by subregional authorities which built upon favourable regional legislation. This category includes Gipuzkoa Provincial Council (GPC), Bizkaia Provincial Council (BPC), the municipality of Manresa, Gwynedd Council from 1993 onwards and, to a much lesser extent, Isle of Anglesey County Council (ACC). They all share the characteristic of having engaged in internal language policy, having built upon permissive general guidelines outlined in regional legislation. In the case of the two Basque provincial councils, legislation in the form of the Normalization of the Use of Basque Law 1982 and the Civil Service Laws of 1989 and 1997 legitimate the development of language requirements for a percentage of staff based on the demolinguistic constitution of any given administrative territory (Agirreazkuenaga, 2005).

However, two points need to be made at this juncture. First, both GPC and BPC have been able to take advantage of these regional enactments in order to achieve significant gains in their internal administrations which had previously functioned, to all intents and purposes, through Spanish only. And secondly, the provincial councils are not required to engage substantially with LP *per se* since it is not within their original responsibilities, but the fact that they have done so, and the *modus operandi* used to this end, is worthy of further reflection.

The first LP steps taken by the two councils were the creation of internal language promotion directorates, in 1991 in GPC and 1998 in the case of BPC. A higher percentage of Basque speakers within the GPC workforce, and the fact that Gipuzkoa-elected members had accorded internal political recognition of LP measures at an earlier stage than in Bizkaia, has led to the Council taking a maximalist interpretation of the abovementioned regional legislation through the passing of an internal regulation (Gipuzkoa Provincial Council, 2004). This is an example of subregional government building on permissive regional legislation both in its LP objectives and their continued implementation. The 1982 language law refers only to the fact that Basque is the autochthonous language for the autonomous community and does not stipulate how this will be implemented in any of its public administrations. The aforementioned 1989 law builds on the 1982 legislation by denoting a framework and corresponding timescale with which to achieve the stated aim of working internally through Basque.

With the stated aim of creating a fully bilingual workforce built upon pragmatism, GPC goes a step further than both regional laws through the development of three categories of "bilingual administrative units" (Gipuzkoa Provincial Council, 2004) and a parallel staff release scheme for intensive language learning.[5] When measured against the regional government formula based on a mathematical-territorial requirement for a set number of bilingual staff to correspond to any given administrative catchment area, the requirement which GPC places upon its staff to comply with a certain language competence is greater than that of the Basque Government (Amundarain, 2005: 37).

Although internal LP actions began later in Bizkaia than in Gipuzkoa, the same general objective prevails, although the internal administrative method for reaching the stated objective and time-scales are different. For example, BPC has not yet passed an internal regulation promoting Basque but rather has implemented the Basque Government's Language Normalization Plans for its own purposes. Whilst not using internal mandates, the BPC Normalization Plan shares a similar three-category "bilingual administrative units" model with language skilling occurring as part of staff release schemes. The expenditure is not inconsiderable. For example, 85 870 hours were devoted in 1999–2000 to staff language skilling (Bizkaia Provincial Council, 2005). The BPC is an example of subregional government which engages in LP once it has the political will, and the green light, from the regional tier to do so.

However, perhaps the most striking example within the case studies of subregional government which has judiciously waited for the 'green light' of regional legislation in order to legitimate its own LP is the municipality of Manresa. The municipality has overhauled its language policy twice, each time following regional legislative developments. In Manresa, during the first legislature of the Catalan socialists (the PSC), committee meetings were held in Catalan but with attendant internal and public documentation continuing to be created and administered in Spanish (interview with portfolio member, Manresa). However, LP was swiftly reconfigured in 1983 after the first regional language act was passed. With this new act less than a month old, Manresa adopted a policy which made Catalan the default language for its activities and was the first municipality in the autonomous community to do so. LP was again strengthened in 1993, this time when the town hall was under the control of the CiU (*Convergència i Unió*, Convergence and Union; centre-right nationalists), following local government legislation passed by the Catalan Government which had bolstered the use of Catalan as the internal language and default language of use with third-party service providers (Ajuntament de Manresa, 1993).

Reluctant LP

Although Isle of Anglesey County Council can be listed among those subregional governments which have built upon regional legislation, a substantial caveat needs to be put against its LP activity since 1996 when it came into existence, previously having been part of a larger Gwynedd County Council. Following both reorganization and the WLA of 1993, a number of elected members and officers who had been previously socialized in the working practices of Gwynedd County Council, ideologically driven in favour of normalizing the use of Welsh in its internal practices, were now at the helm of a smaller unitary authority. Indeed, the language of the Senior Management Team changed overnight to Welsh as did the Executive (interview with executive officer, ACC). Interview data, however, show that although some ACC departments use Welsh as the language of work, the stated aim of Welsh being the main language of internal administration has since atrophied in a council where the overwhelming majority of officers and elected members speak Welsh (Isle of Anglesey County Council, 2001). This can be accounted for in terms of a gradual distancing between LP and political priorities on the island: "Politically, there was a staggering lack of vision. A golden opportunity presented itself to make a difference, to take a lead nationally, and this has been squandered." (Interview with ex-senior policy officer, 2007).

All three orientations mentioned above speak to subregional government being a relevant governance tier in internal LP, having either furrowed a distinctive path before the enactment of regional legislation or having made discursive and strategic use of it. Nevertheless, regional statutory provisions cannot on their own account fully for the diversity of subregional activity. Neither can they reveal initial and continuing reasons for engaging with LP or indeed disengaging from it. The presumption, however, that subregional government is an acquiescent handmaiden which merely implements regional legislative drivers and policy steers may be discarded. The following section argues that demolinguistic considerations, conceptual development of language legislation as well as fiscal provisions can help to better account for the diversity across the case studies. However, in order to understand fully the degree of subregional engagement and disengagement with LP practices, party political dynamics within the regional system require analysis.

Demolinguistic Considerations

In terms of the percentage of those in the autonomous community with self-ascribed knowledge of the language, Catalan is not, strictly speaking, a minority language (Statistical Institute of Catalonia, 2012). The situation in the Basque Country and Wales is significantly different as regards levels of knowledge and use of the autochthonous language (Jones, 2012; Basque Government, 2005). Moreover, the linguistic proximity between Catalan and Spanish means that it is easier for government agencies to deploy human and financial resources more efficiently in the task of promoting linguistic competence among non-Catalan speakers than is the case of Wales and the Basque Country. Demolinguistics thus have a significant explanatory force, yet can change over time. Intralinguistic proximity, however, cannot be readily impacted upon.

Conceptual Development of Language Legislation

The first linguistic norm to secure protection in the fledgling democracy of Spain was regional co-officiality of the autochthonous language enshrined in the Constitution. Following the arrival of regional statutes for both Catalonia and the Basque Country in 1979, the non-statewide language was identified as each region's *lengua propia*, its 'autochthonous' language. Conceptual and practical implications around the autochthonous language under such a definition currently coalesce around the following:

- the linkages between the non-statewide language and a specific territory, thus initiating a process whereby linguistic rights of the citizen are recognized and maintained (Vernet Llobet and Pou Pujolràs, 2006);
- the reinforcement of the use of non-statewide language in regional public administrations;
- the extension of the concept of *lengua propia* in order to prioritize, or in the case of the Autonomous Community of the Basque Country (ACBC), to pave the way for a prioritization of, the non-statewide language in specific contexts (Agirreazkuenaga, 2005: 19).

There is, nevertheless, considerable difference in the interpretation of *lengua propia* in the two regions, arising clearly due to their demolinguistic differences. In Catalonia the concept is synonymous with setting language requirements for virtually all public administration positions. In the Basque Country, the concept has been operationalized by way of a mathematical-bureaucratic arrangement which increases the percentage of linguistic requirements within public office over time in accordance with local demographics. Despite the difference in interpretation of *lengua propia*, the concept in both regions has paved the way for subsequent legislation to cumulatively build on primary language legislation.

Conceptual factors shaping regional and subregional LP in Wales are of a different order. Perhaps the most prevalent consideration is the hitherto lack of regional language legislation providing official status for Welsh within a declaratory statement, similar to that incorporated within the concept of *lengua propia*.[6] Before the 2011 language legislation, it was not possible to constitute and validate a conceptual domain for the language which could be implemented practically on a territorial basis.[7] Previous language legislation, in the form of the Welsh Language Act 1993, related to neo-liberal notions around the promotion of Welsh and enablement of bilingual services (Williams and Morris, 2000) rather than the granting of official status. Gwynedd Council, upon local government reorganization in 1996, took advantage of the discourse of enablement contained in WLA 1993 as a hook with which to subsequently legitimate the formulation and development of its LP activities (interview with retired senior executive, 2007).

Fiscal Capacities

Subregional LP activity operates under varied fiscal scenarios. Among the case studies, the fiscal position of the Basque provincial authorities in respect of the Basque government gives them increased political leverage since they are responsible for regulating, levying and administering 94% of all taxes collected in the community (Novo Arbona, 2010). Two budgetary developments from the late 1990s should focus our attention: expenditure on LP activity in Gipuzkoa and Bizkaia as a percentage of global provincial expenditure as well as the year-on-year increase in LP expenditure. These contributions are either above or close to the percentage expenditure of 0.7% which the regional government designated for aggregate LP expenditures as a percentage of global spends across all tiers of government in the autonomous community if language policy is to be made sustainable (Mateo, 2005: 15). Notwithstanding the fact that the provincial councils are not legally required to be LP actors, the fact that both have not only initiated grant allocation to town halls in their territory in order to sustain LP goals, but that they also co-ordinate this process through a regional government-established network would put in doubt the viability of understanding regional LP using a purely top-down analysis.

Welsh local authorities and municipalities in Catalonia do not enjoy such a privileged arrangement. The percentage of LP expenditure by subregional governments in both regions is, therefore, significantly lower than that of the provincial authorities. For example, Gwynedd Council LP expenditure was 0.2% of the global spend[8] in 2006. In the case of Santa Coloma de Gramenet, the corresponding figure in 2006 was 0.18% (Consorci de Normalització Lingüística L'Heura, 2006).

Across the regions, therefore, subregional LP fiscal *capacity* is influenced by differing budgeting regimes. A quick comparison across the regions concentrates the mind: the internal and external LP of the subregional GPC and BPC spend in 2006 came to €14.9 million (Bizkaia Provincial Council, 2006; Gipuzkoa Provincial Council, 2006), whereas in the same period the Welsh Assembly Government deployed £13.4 million towards *regional* LP activities (Welsh Assembly Government, 2007), despite both regions showing not wholly dissimilar demolinguistic features. The above demolinguistic, legislative and fiscal factors, however, can only be read off a larger script, and they lead to a more complex question: why do subregional entities engage with LP activity in the first place? An analysis of the regional political system offers a more comprehensive backdrop with which to frame the impact of the significant yet epiphenomenal factors discussed above.

The Regional Institutional and Party System

In his study on Basque nationalism, Jan Mansvelt Beck (2005) describes the Basque autonomous community as a weak proto-state due to the complex and antagonistic relationship between the hitherto incumbent Christian democrat PNV (*Partido Nacionalista Vasco*, Basque Nationalist Party) and anti-systemic nationalist groupings. Extending his analysis, he concludes that autonomous communities "have become a new setting in which to develop alternative policies and practices" (Mansvelt Beck, 2005: 154). Chris Ross (1996: 488) takes a similar position on Basque and Catalan nationalism: "The regional party systems will continue to act as an important dimension of the changing relationship between center and periphery, long recognized as crucial to the development of nationalism for the latter".

Turning to regional LP, the ethnologist Jacqueline Urla (1993: 818) states that planning for language is not a 'natural' outgrowth of nationalism. Rather, this activity is carved out. Urla refers to the use of statistics by the civil service of the Basque Government during the first years of the new autonomous community, with the express intent of presenting data about Basque speakers and communities as part of a contestation around political ideologies. This article argues, however, that literatures dealing with LP have not fully recognized the regional political system "in its entirety", and that a wider understanding of the intergovernmental nature of the regional institutional and party political system needs to be developed. In each of the three regions, engagement with LP by nationalist parties is first analysed, before focusing on LP engagements by unionist parties.

A trend which would be expected is for nationalist parties to claim action on behalf of the autochthonous language within party policy and work programmes. If political support for LP is secured within the region's institutions, such a claim could then be revealed in the public domain as transparent language planning. If no such policy support is secured, then a more opaque version of language planning will obtain. Although a party's unionism manifests itself differently under the prevailing socio-political circumstances (Guibernau, 2004), unionist parties would not be expected to put as much emphasis on LP as a 'core' priority, highlighting rather rhetorical support or degrees of opposition. The task now is to apply these expectations to the reality of the three regions.

Autonomous Community of the Basque Country

Hegemonic political power within the ACBC since the restoration of democracy has been vested in the Christian democrat nationalists of the PNV (de Pablo and Mees,

2005). From 1980 until 2009, the PNV either held total control of the regional executive or was the majority partner in coalition governments. In general elections since 1977, it has all but once received the largest share of votes. In provincial elections in Gipuzkoa and Bizkaia, where the overwhelming majority of the population of the autonomous community reside, it has controlled the executive or been the majority partner in coalition formations. Despite being the hegemon among nationalist voters, however, this dominance has been far from universal.

During the first 20 years of the democratic period, the party had never managed to generate more than two-thirds of all nationalist votes cast, the rest being taken by the social democratic EA (*Eusko Alkartasuna*, Basque Solidarity) and the pro-independence *Batasuna*, which was banned in 2003 and then legalized in 2011 when it entered into electoral coalitions with other nationalist formations, including EA. Language promotion is considered a significant policy driver when claiming nationalist credentials (Morán, 2004: 119), heightening the role accorded to the Basque language within the long-established duality inside the PNV between those in favour of Basque regional governance developed within the current constitutional framework and those in favour of a Basque governance scenario which goes beyond the current arrangements (de Pablo and Mees, 2005).

The main priority of the PNV in the new democratic period has been the strengthening of regional institutions and campaigning against efforts by the two major state parties to limit the power of "fast lane" autonomous communities (Pérez-Nievas, 2002). As part of these efforts, restoration of the fiscal 'historic rights' of the Basque provinces became a core PNV claim, leading to tension within the party at a territorial level and across Basque governance (Mees, 2003). Provincial fiscal power is thus currently privileged over the patriation of such power to the regional government. With fiscal arrangements in place, an element in the PNV's vision for nation-building has been LP activities. This was initiated at the regional level and then engaged at the subregional level. Most primary and secondary LP legislation had come into force during the first ten years of PNV control.

Another LP tool during the past decade has been the general language strategy of the Basque Government. Before the change of government in 2009, this example of non-legislative consensuated 'soft law', developed during the particularly tense period of the Lizarra–Estella Agreement, may have been favoured by the PNV because it did not involve recourse to negotiations as a precursor to legislation with a non-nationalist pole which was increasing in strength. Whilst the PNV at the regional level may have been interested in keeping language a 'non-issue' (de la Calle and Miley, 2008: 710), and whilst keeping in mind once again Basque demolinguistic realities, evidence from other levels of the regional system would suggest that language is indeed 'an issue' with both concrete and conceptual implications and that this has been either PNV-driven or been consensuated by the party in Bizkaia and Gipuzkoa.

At the subregional level, the PNV has chosen two different LP paths in the two provincial councils, passing internal provincial decrees in Gipuzkoa while adopting in Bizkaia a language plan which builds on the foundations of the regional language strategy. However, despite the use of provincial decrees on the one hand and regional soft law on the other, there has been considerable internal doubt and tension within the PNV regarding these activities. This has led to political ambiguity and decisions whereby, for example, LP activity carried out by Bizkaia has not been fully accounted for:

> [our language policy] . . . that's a whole history of events which hasn't completely reached the public domain—it's our internal history, if you will. You will see in our documentation why our Basque Promotion Directorate was established in September 1999, but you will not find any reference anywhere as to why it was created. That is something which has never gone on public record, and I have my doubts as to whether it ever will do so. Who is to say that language isn't the co-responsibility of both the Basque Government and BPC? (Interview with senior executive officer, BPC)

It may be that part of the reason for this ambiguity is the unstable relationship between the PNV and the anti-systemic Batasuna. Engagement with LP is thus connected to tactical decisions to attract nationalist votes as well as being associated with the party's core commitment on the issue of promoting Basque. Of interest is the fact that, in 1992, according to a regional government language policy officer, no LP activity existed in the PNV-controlled provincial councils (Tejerina, 1992), a statement which in itself is not surprising since LP as a core responsibility does not rest with provincial councils. However, the subregional move by Gipuzkoa and Bizkaia to embrace LP activity could be understood as coinciding with a regional shift of power towards the end of the 1990s within the PNV towards a more sovereign-based orientation (Pérez-Nievas, 2002). LP in Gipuzkoa and Bizkaia over the last ten years, in this light, thus forms an important, yet mainly unaccounted for part of a nation-building process. If this is the case, then a further question should be asked: is this activity unaccounted for because it occurs at the subregional level?

If the intra-nationalist relationship described above feeds into LP decision making, then this is also the case for unionist parties within the regional institutional system, specifically the Basque Socialists (PSE, *Partido Socialista de Euskadi*, Basque Socialist Party). The commitment of the PNV to LP is highlighted in legislation around the Basque language, a language strategy which received majority approval within the regional legislature as well as an increase in LP activity in the provincial councils. Yet these actions have been limited in two ways—in the first instance, by demolinguistic considerations and, secondly, by the weight of the PSE. Although this party did not achieve control of the regional executive until 2009, it has garnered the second highest number of votes cast in both general and regional elections, despite its influence at provincial level being less pronounced. In the first legislature after the restoration of democracy, the PSE emphasized a class-based discourse whilst accepting significant decentralization.

However, both deepening political violence and the embedding of regional structures soon led to a change of course for the Basque socialists, particularly after its sister party, the statewide PSOE (*Partido Socialista Obrero Español*, Spanish Socialist Workers' Party), gained power in Madrid in 1982. With PSE efforts to reduce the power bases of the new regional and provincial council structures, class-based rhetoric began to embrace stronger versions of unionist anti-regionalism (Pérez-Nievas, 2002). By the early 1990s, Tejerina (1992) shows that a considerable number of citizens of the autonomous community were of the opinion that the PSE had ceased to be a party which was proactive in promoting Basque. Careful and tentative stewardship of the 1982 language act through the regional legislature (Etxenike, 2002) had by 1998 given way to PSE disagreement concerning the regional language strategy in 1998 (Basque Parliament, 1999). The Basque regional institutional and party system is thus characterized by significant disagreement between the major nationalist and unionist forces on the degree of the promotion of Basque.

Autonomous Community of Catalonia

On the issue of LP, compared to the Basque Country, Catalonia's political system in the democratic period has experienced wider consensual agreement among nationalist parties as well as those parties incorporating significant unionist elements. Regional LP has been driven mainly by one regional political party, CiU, which governed either through majority or in coalition between 1980 and 2003. This federated alliance, consisting of two distinct parties, was created in 1978 in order to provide a nationalist 'backbone' to the politics of Catalonia (Barberà and Barrio, 2006). Combining liberal and Christian democratic trends, its ideological reach has been able to engage a large swathe of electoral opinion. In this light, policy development and delivery have been aligned to nation-building (Baras and Dalmeses, 1998), within which LP processes form a significant part.

Engagement between left-wing parties in Catalonia and nation-building aspirations also form a backdrop to LP. During the change from autarchy into democratic structures, the now defunct United Socialist Party of Catalonia (PSUC) became a powerful political force in densely populated municipalities around Barcelona, including Santa Coloma de Gramenet (Ubach and Fabà, 1997: 255). The pro-independence leftist *Esquerra Republicana de Catalunya* (ERC, Republican Left of Catalonia) is also a significant force in the regional system. These three Catalonia-relevant parties—CiU, ERC and PSUC—have proven to be influential in the implementation of regional and subregional LP.

The 1983 regional language law became the main legitimizing element for regional and subregional LP. Although general agreement was obtained across the parties that legislation was required to stabilize the use of Catalan, CiU's influence on the law's contents, the media campaign by the regional government in its initial rolling out as well as subordinate legislation which followed it, was substantial (Argelaguet, 1998). The main planks of the 1983 law were revisited in the 1998 Language Policy Law when CiU seized the opportunity when the central conservative PP (*Partido Popular*, People's Party) government depended on CiU policy support in Madrid. This legislation was pushed through the Catalan legislature despite opposition from the PSC who were becoming increasingly vocal about the need to slow down the promotion of Catalan and from the ERC, who felt that it did not go far enough (Costa, 2003: 413).

The Secretariat for Language Policy was given full rein to draw up a new law and "everything else could wait, including the continued promotion of Catalan in the municipalities" (interview with ex-CiU political appointee, 2007). CiU was able to frame its version of the legislation as the most acceptable option to both nationalist forces and the business sector which secured a sizeable reduction in the remit of the 1998 Law (Boix-Fuster, 2004: 35). At this point, as Roller (2001: 39) notes, "the 1998 Linguistic Law marked the end of an era of consensual politics in the area of linguistic policy". This is attested to by a senior town hall representative dealing with language policy, "With one fell swoop, the nationalist government decided to bring down all that was consensual about the language policy" (interview, 2007).

LP activity in Catalan municipalities, however, rests overwhelmingly with non-nationalist forces. Here the term 'non-nationalist' is used due to disagreement about the extent to whether the Catalan socialists from the PSC, can be defined as unionists (Sintes, 2001). The orientation and internal make-up of the PSC along the state–sub-state cleavage can be problematized across periods of time and according to geography. This ambiguity is summed up in the term *catalanisme*, the socio-cultural ontological contents of which remain a subject of keen debate in Catalonia (Marfany, 1996). However, the PSC, more than any other party, can lay claim to having implemented regional language legislation at a municipal level, as alluded to by Chris Ross (1996: 488): "In the initial Catalan party system the PSC and PSUC were thus themselves important vehicles of national feeling and not, as in the case of Basque Socialists, a key negative referent for nationalists."

At the beginning of the democratic period, the regional institutional system of Catalonia, with its nationalist and *catalanista* parties, was developing into an increasingly uniform system in terms of increasing the sense of sub-state nationhood. Ross (1996: 488), again, is pertinent:

> In 1980 in the Catalan system, the strength of national feeling was not measured by the 37 per cent of votes won jointly by the CiU and the ERC. Instead, it was reflected in the approximately 80% share of parties positively disposed towards the idea of Catalan nationhood, including those of the Left, a proportion of which by 1984 had risen to almost 90 per cent.

This is reflected in the significant changes brought by the LP programme during the first legislature of the PSUC-led town hall of SCG and supported by the PSC. Political parties, however, do not remain static and the past 15 years have seen variations within PSC support for LP intervention at both the regional (Roller, 2001: 39; Argelaguet, 2007: 170–171) and subregional level (interview with SCG policy officer, 2007).

Wales

The constitutional make-up of the UK within which LP operates in Wales, that of a customary yet increasingly explicit legal tradition (Johnson, 2004), is significantly different at first sight from that of Spain. Planning for the increased use of Welsh can be interpreted within "the tradition of British constitutional adhocery" (Laffin and Thomas, 1999: 89). In accordance with such a vision, although the Welsh regional system has quickly embedded itself within an increasingly asymmetrical UK governance framework, the central state continues to execute "an important gatekeeper role" in the intergovernmental relationship between the centre and the Welsh executive and legislature (Wyn Jones and Scully, 2008: 207). At the party level, Wales cannot now be considered to be a one-party unionist system and, from among the four major parties in the emerging regional system, Plaid Cymru is the party which appeals most to the Welsh electorate as "a party of greater relevance to Wales" (Wyn Jones and Scully, 2006: 190).

With the devolution settlement barely out if its first decade, Plaid Cymru only recently accessed the regional executive as a junior coalition partner (Elias, 2009: 113). The governing Welsh Labour Party may in future be seen to be vulnerable as the Welsh regional institutional system deepens (Bradbury, 2010: 726), due to tensions between those in the party sceptical or in favour of the direction of the two constitutional settlements since 1998. Although the party, Laffin *et al.* (2003: 53) suggest, are now afforded more policy discretion "to respond to the political environment in Wales", other commentators have noted that this discretion has not yet been actioned, despite the development of the regional system putting further pressure on party policy "which has arguably been demonstrating the intellectual atrophy that is characteristic of one-partyism" (Wyn Jones and Scully, 2008: 207).

Such is the current regional backdrop for LP in Wales. In this emerging regional system, the "exclusive prerogative of specific political positions" around LP has been considered by some as harmful to the long-term prospects of Welsh (Williams, G. 2007: 302). Undoubtedly, Plaid Cymru is the inheritor of such a positioning. It is too early to report on the regional system's response to the new Welsh Language Measure passed in 2011, yet it would appear that other Welsh political parties have responded to Plaid Cymru reaching the threshold of governing by refashioning policy programmes, for example on language, to garner a more "Welsh face" for electoral purposes (Elias, 2009: 113). However, regional LP is also beholden to the particular essence of pre-devolution legislation in the form of the WLA of 1993 which was sculpted by regional Conservative elites and accepted meekly by a weakened central Conservative Party (Edwards *et al.*, 2011). As the concept of the official status of the Welsh language was not enshrined in the 1993 act, the Assembly Government's national language strategy was also considered to suffer from a lack of conceptual clarity (Roddick, 2007) until the official nature of Welsh was more explicitly stated in the 2011 measure.

At the subregional level, Plaid Cymru in 1974 took advantage of the waning of the Labour Party in the north-west to take control of the county council, embarking on a programme of constantly evolving LP activities in those Welsh-speaking communities that were so emblematic to the original ethos of the party and its supporters (Edwards, 2011). Thomas (1997: 323) paints a picture of "pragmatic tailoring" within Plaid Cymru, considered vague on the language question nationally due to efforts to widen the party base territorially, whilst LP activity in Gwynedd is the direct result of the deepening influence of Plaid Cymru in the organizational and linguistic practices of the local authority.

Due to the absence of a centrally driven LP policy in pre-devolution Wales, Plaid Cymru in Gwynedd worked on a relative *tabula rasa*, taking gradual but purposeful steps towards the legitimation of Welsh as the main language of internal administration, increased bilingual education provision as well as attempting to exert an influence over public institutions within the county. Some aspects of this activity, especially outside the realm of statutory education, have not been given due public scrutiny. However, a counterfactual exercise might result in the presumption that such reticence to full disclosure of LP activities might have been less pronounced were mechanisms in place linking local LP activity more implicitly with the Welsh Office. Following the legitimation inherent in the language legislation of 1993, Gwynedd within a few years revisited previous internal LP activity, making Welsh the default language of internal operations (Gwynedd Council, 1996).

The influence of Plaid Cymru within Gwynedd Council suggests that the politics of language in north-west Wales is mobilized around the influence of the nationalist party. Van Morgan's model of the politicization of language at the regional level in Galicia and Wales (Van Morgan, 2006: 451) suggests that solidarity and collective identity can feed into such a politicization. The intergovernmental interactions and transactions of the regional system, including subregional government, can help expand such a model as it attempts to map out how solidarity and collective identity are woven around language claims. However, more research is needed to understand how the politicization of language is engaged by the regional institutional and political system in its totality.

Concluding Remarks

This article demonstrates the linkages between subregional language policies, their legitimization by sub-state political parties, as well as their location within, and impact upon, regional governance. Literature on comparative subregional LP remains scant and unproblematized, yet the focus here on the language policy interventions conducted by six subregional governments within three regionalizing polities serves to highlight the values regional political parties accord the knowledge of, and use of, non-statewide languages. Albeit within differing governance systems, subregional governments in the Basque Country, Catalonia and Wales have been responsible for significant LP interventions and, in a number of cases, have acted virtually independently of the regional governance structures, as in the case of Gwynedd Council before local government reorganization in 1996. In the Basque Country, the tax-raising capabilities of both the provincial authorities of Gipuzkoa and Bizkaia have facilitated significant LP investment and innovation, despite the fact that LP does not constitute a core provincial authority responsibility. In Catalonia, early LP interventions by Santa Coloma de Gramenet municipality predated both regional language and local administration legislation. All of these examples highlight the LP footprint of subregional authorities within regionalizing systems and implicitly invoke the LP values of regional political parties.

Political parties are core organizational actors within liberal democracy, and one of the most prominent features of any system is the type of party politics which unfolds there (Wyn Jones and Scully, 2008: 207). It thus seems coherent that literature dealing with non-statewide LP should take into account the totality of the actors involved in the regional system, as subregional LP feeds into party political strategies for regional empowerment. Although it is not always clear what the criteria for LP success are, what is evident is that locating and tracking subregional LP within the wider regional system is essential to an increased understanding of how individual and group language claims are identified and promoted. LP engagement by six subregional authorities in the Basque Country, Catalonia and Wales bear witness to the interplay between converging and diverging visions of democracy and identity, as well as to the political parties which interpret and refashion the products of this interplay.

Notes

[1]These are, in the Basque Country, Gipuzkoa Provincial Council (GPC) and Bizkaia Provincial Council (BPC); in Catalonia, the municipalities of Manresa and Santa Coloma de Gramenet (SCG); and in Wales, Gwynedd Council and the Isle of Anglesey County Council (ACC).

[2]Given the particularity of each case study area as well as the multiple subregional levels of government, the election criteria for the case studies were threefold: multi-functionality of service provision; population size in receipt of subregional provision (>60 000); census percentage stating knowledge of the non-statewide language (>20%).

[3]Although statistics for 1981 show knowledge of Welsh at 63% for Gwynedd (Jones, 2012) and knowledge of Catalan at 50.3% for SCG (Government of Catalonia, 2012), the percentage level of *use* of Catalan is much lower than the corresponding usage level in Gwynedd. This would suggest that demolinguistic factors are not the only ones at play when making LP decisions.

[4]All interview translations are my own.

[5]As a precursor to implementation of the bilingual units, between 1992 and 1996, 400 staff—approximately a quarter of the GPC workforce—were released for this purpose on full pay with replacement staff taking their positions for periods of up to two years (interview with language promotion directorate officer, GPC).

[6]Part I of the Welsh Language (Wales) Measure 2011 provides for the official status of the Welsh Language.

[7]It could be argued that the Welsh Language (Wales) Measure 2011 provides for such a territorial development, for example at 44(2).

[8]This figure (£340 000) is derived from adding translation requirements to the posts of internal language trainer and language officer.

References

Agirreazkuenaga, I. (2005), El euskara en el marco del autogobierno: propuestas del futuro, *Revista Vasca de Administración Pública*, Vol.73, No.2, pp.19–31.

Agranoff, R. (2010), *Local Governments and their Intergovernmental Networks in Federalizing Spain*. Montreal: McGill-Queen's University Press.

Ajuntament de Manresa (1993), *Reglament per a l'ús de la Llengua Catalana a l'Ajuntament de Manresa*. Manresa: Ajuntament de Manresa.

Amundarain, J. (2005), Euskararen erabileraren normalizazioa Gipuzkoako Foru Aldundian, *Bat Soziolinguistika Aldizkaria*, Vol.55, No.2, pp.37–51.

Argelaguet, J. (1998), *El procés d'elaboració de la Llei de Política Lingüística*. Barcelona: Mediterrània.

Argelaguet, J. (2007), La qüestió llingüística en els primers passos del procès de reforma de l'Estatut d'autonomia de Catalunya, *Revista de Llengua i Dret*, No.47, pp.145–183.

Baras, M. and Matas Dalmeses, J. (1998), Els partits polítics i el sistema de partits, in M. Caminal Badia and J. Matas Dalmases (eds), *El Sistema Polític de Catalunya*. Barcelona: Universitat de Barcelona.

Barberà, O. and Barrio, A. (2006), Convergència i Unió: from Stability to Decline?, in L. De Winter, M. Gómez-Reino and P. Lynch (eds), *Autonomist Parties in Europe: Identity Politics and the Revival of the Territorial Cleavage*. Barcelona: ICPS.

Basque Government (2005), *III Mapa Soziolinguistikoa*. Vitoria-Gasteiz: Eusko Jaurlaritza.

Basque Parliament (1999), *Bilkura-Egunkaria: 1999ko abenduaren 10ean egindako osoko bilkura*. Available at http://www.parlamento.euskadi.net/pdfdocs/publi/2/06/000037.pdf (accessed 10 December 2012).

Bizkaia Provincial Council (2005), *Bizkaiko Foru Aldundiaren 2005eko maiatzaren 3ko Erabakia; izan ere, beraren bidez xedatu da Bizkaiko foru aldundiaren euskararen erabilera normalizatzeko 2003–2007ko epealdirako plana onestea*. Available at http://www.bizkaia.net/lehendakaritza/Bao_bob/2005/05/20050512a089.pdf#page=4 (accessed 10 December 2012).

Bizkaia Provincial Council (2006), *2006ko Aurrekontu Orokorren Aurkezpena*. Bilbao: Bizkaiko Foru Aldundia.

Boix-Fuster, E. (2004), Poder i llengües a Catalunya, *Revista Catalana de Sociologia*, No.20, pp.35–55.

Bradbury, J. (2010), Wales and the 2010 General Election. *Parliamentary Affairs*, Vol.63, No.4, pp.726–741.

Cole, A. (2006), *Beyond Devolution and Decentralisation: Building Regional Capacity in Wales and Brittany*. Manchester: Manchester University Press.

Consorci de Normalització Llingüística L'Heura (2006), Memòria, Barcelona: Unpublished material.

Costa, J. (2003), Catalan Linguistic Policy: Liberal or Illiberal?, *Nations and Nationalism*, Vol.9, No.3, pp.413–432.

de la Calle, L. and Miley, T. J. (2008), Is There More Assimilation in Catalonia than in the Basque Country? Analysing Dynamics of Assimilation in Nationalist Contexts, *European Journal of Political Research*, No.47, pp.710–736.

de Pablo, S. and Mees, L. (2005), *El Péndulo Patriótico. Historia del PNV, 1895–2005*. Barcelona: Crítica.

de Winter, L. and Türsan, H. (eds) (1998), *Regionalist Parties in Western Europe*. London: Routledge.

Edwards, A. (2011), *Labour's crisis: Plaid Cymru, the Conservatives, and the Decline of the Labour Party in North-west Wales, 1960–1974*. Cardiff: University of Wales Press.

Edwards, A., Tanner, D. and Carlin, P. (2011), The Conservative Governments and the Development of Welsh Language Policy in the 1980s, *The Historical Journal*, Vol.54, No.2, pp.529–551.

Elias, A. (2009), Plaid Cymru and the Challenges of Adopting to Post-Devolution Wales, *Contemporary Wales*, No.22, pp.113–141.

Etxenike, P. M. (2002), Un marco jurídico sustentado en el consenso, *II Jornadas de Reflexiones Sociales. El proceso de normalización del uso del euskera*. Vitoria-Gasteiz, Fundación Fernando Buesa, 3 December.

Gipuzkoa Provincial Council (2004), *Aldundi Elebidun Bat: una diputación bilingüe*. Donostia: Gipuzkoako Foru Aldundia.

Gipuzkoa Provincial Council (2006), 2006ko Aurrekontuak: Euskara, San Sebastián: Unpublished Material.

Government of Catalonia (2012), *Població segons coneixement del* català. Santa Coloma de Gramenet: Generalitat de CatalunyaAvailable at http://www.idescat.net/territ/BasicTerr?TC=5&V0=1&V1=08245&V3=876&V4=17&ALLINFO=TRUE&PARENT=25&CTX=B (accessed 10 December 2012).

Guibernau, M. (2004), *Catalan Nationalism: Francoism, Transition, and Democracy*. London: Routledge.

Gwynedd Council (1996), Cyfarfod 19eg Gorffennaf yr Is-bwyllgor Iaith, Caernarfon: Unpublished material.

Hepburn, E. (2009), Re-conceptualizing Sub-state Mobilization, *Regional and Federal Studies*, Vol.19, Nos.4–5, pp.477–499.

Isle of Anglesey County Council (2001), Report on Implementation of Language Scheme 2000–2001, Llangefni: Unpublished material.

Johnson, N. (2004), *Reshaping the British Constitution: Essays in Political Interpretation*. Basingstoke: Palgrave.

Jones, H. (2012) *A Statistical Overview of the Welsh Language*. Cardiff: Welsh Language Board.

Laffin, M. and Thomas, A. (1999), The United Kingdom: Federalism in Denial? *Publius*, Vol.29, No.3, pp.89–107.

Laffin, M., Taylor, G. and Thomas, A. (2003), Devolution and Party Organization: The Case of the Wales Labour Party, *Contemporary Wales*, No.16, pp.53–73.

Lo Bianco, J. (2004), Language Planning as Applied Linguistics, in A. Davies and C. Elder (eds), *The Handbook of Applied Linguistics*. Oxford: Blackwell.

Mansvelt Beck, J. (2005), *Territory and Power: Conflicting Nationalisms in the Basque Country*. London: Routledge.

Marfany, J.-L. (1996), *La Cultura del Catalanisme*. Barcelona: Empúries.

Mateo, M. (2005), Language Policy and Planning of the Status of Basque, 1: the Basque Autonomous Community (BAC), *International Journal of the Sociology of Language*, No.174, pp.9–23.

McLeod, W. (1998), Autochthonous Language Communities and the Race Relations Act, *Web Journal of Current Legal Issues*. Available at http://webjcli.ncl.ac.uk/1998/issue1/mcleod1.html (accessed 10 December 2012).

Mees, L. (2003), *Nationalism, Violence and Democracy: The Basque Clash of Identities*. Basingstoke: Palgrave.

Morán, S. (2004), *PNV-ETA: Historia de una relación imposible*. Madrid: Tecnos.

Notícias Jurídicas (2012), *Ley 8/1987, de 15 de abril, Municipal y de Régimen Local de Cataluña*. Available at http://noticias.juridicas.com/base_datos/CCAA/ca-l8-1987.t1.html (accessed 10 December 2012).

Novo Arbona, A. (2010), *La excepcionalidad del modelo federal foral vasco*. Valencia: Tirant Lo Blanch.

Pérez-Nievas, S. (2002), *Modelo de partido y cambio político. El Partido Nacionalista Vasco en el proceso de transición y consolidación democrática en el País Vasco*. Madrid: Instituto Juan March.

Roddick, W. (2007), One Nation-Two Voices: The Welsh Language in the Governance of Wales, in C. Williams (ed.), *Language and Governance*. Cardiff: University of Wales Press.

Roller, E. (2001), The 1997 *Llei del Català*: A Pandora's Box in Catalonia? *Regional and Federal Studies*, Vol.11, No.1, pp.39–54.

Ross, C. (1996), Nationalism and Party Competition in the Basque Country and Catalonia, *West European Politics*, Vol.19, No.3, pp.488–506.

Ruiz Amendral, V. (2003), The Asymmetric Distribution of Taxation Powers in the Spanish State of Autonomies: The Common System and the Foral Tax regimes, *Regional and Federal Studies*, Vol.13, No.4, pp.41–66.

Shadow Gwynedd County Council (1973a), Cofnodion 30ain Mai y Gweithgor Polisi Dwyieithog, Caernarfon: Unpublished material.

Shadow Gwynedd County Council (1973b), Cofnodion 25ain Mai y Pwyllgor Llywio, Caernarfon: Unpublished material.

Sintes, M. (2001), *Què Pensa Ernest Lluch*. Barcelona: Dèria.

Statistical Institute of Catalonia (2012), *Coneixement del català. Per nivells de coneixement*. Available at http://www.idescat.cat/pub/?id=aec&n=887 (accessed 10 December 2012).

Tejerina, B. (1992), *Nacionalismo y Lengua: Los Procesos de Cambio Lingüística en el País Vasco*. Madrid: Centro de Investigaciones Sociológicas.

Thomas, A. (1997), Language Policy and Language in Wales: a Comparative Analysis, *Nations and Nationalism*, Vol.3, No.3, pp.323–344.

Ubach, N. and Fabà, A. (1997), De més verdes en maduren: la situació de la llengua catalana a Santa Coloma de Gramenet, *Revista de Llengua i Dret*, No.28, pp.255–271.

Urla, J. (1993), Cultural Politics in an Age of Statistics: Numbers, Nations and the Making of the Basque Identity, *American Ethnologist*, Vol.20, No.4, pp.818–843.

Van Morgan, S. (2006), Language Politics and Regional Nationalist Mobilization in Galicia and Wales, *Ethnicities*, Vol.6, No.4, pp.451–475.

Vernet Llobet, J. and Pou Pojalràs, A (2006), Derechos y Deberes Lingüísticos en las Comunidades Autónomas con Lengua Propia, in J. Pérez Fernández (ed.), *Estudios Sobre El Estatuto Jurídico de las Lenguas en España*. Barcelona: Atelier.

Welsh Assembly Government (2007), *Iaith Pawb and Welsh Language Scheme Annual Report 2007–08*. Cardiff: Welsh Assembly Government.

Williams, C. (ed.) (2007), *Language and Governance*. Cardiff: University of Wales Press.

Williams, G. (2007), Rebuilding the Celtic Languages, *Contemporary Wales*, No.19, pp.302–304.

Williams, G. and Morris, D. (2000), *Language Planning and Language Use: Welsh in a Global Age*. Cardiff: University of Wales Press.

Wright, S. (2004), *Language Policy and Language Planning: From Nationalism to Globalisation*. Basingstoke: Palgrave.

Wyn Jones, R. and Scully, R. (2006), Devolution and Electoral Politics in Wales, in D. Hough and C. Jeffery (eds), *Devolution and Electoral Politics*. Manchester: Manchester University Press.

Wyn Jones, R. and Scully, R. (2008), The End of One-Partyism? Party Politics in Wales in the Second Decade of Devolution, *Contemporary Wales*, No.21, pp.207–218.

On the Right to Linguistic Survival

HUW LEWIS

Department of International Politics, Aberystwyth University, Aberystwyth, UK

ABSTRACT In recent years, political theorists have begun to grapple with the important normative questions that arise in relation to claims for language rights. This paper will seek to contribute to this ongoing debate by focusing in detail on the issue of linguistic survival. It will consider to what extent the members of a minority language community can demand that they have a right to see their language survive into the future. This question will be considered from two distinct perspectives. First, from an individualist perspective: can the members, as individuals, demand that they have a right to see the language survive? Secondly, from a group perspective: can the members, as a collective, demand that they have a right to see the language survive? In both instances it will be demonstrated that the concept of survival raises a number of substantial normative and ontological problems; ones that mean that a right to such a good would be extremely difficult to justify. Given this, it is concluded that those linguistic activists who have tended to base their rights claims on the concept of survival need to reflect critically on their arguments and develop a new conceptual vocabulary.

Introduction

During the nineteenth and the early part of the twentieth centuries, the accepted view was that the decline of minority languages was something that should be welcomed and even encouraged. This stemmed from the fact that these languages tended to be seen as primitive creations that were completely at odds with the modernist and Darwinian tendencies of the age (Jenkins, 1999; Jenkins and Williams, 2000). Securing development and advancement was the priority, and it was assumed that such aims could be achieved only through the medium of dominant state-wide languages. Seeking to arrest and reverse the decline of anything that stood in the way of this process was deemed irrational (Nelde *et al.*, 1996; Williams and Morris, 2000). However, during the second half of the twentieth century, as numerous linguistic minorities began to mobilize politically, this logic was challenged and the welfare of minority languages came, increasingly, to be recognized as a subject that could not simply be dismissed.

This striking change in attitudes has meant that, over the past few decades, the concerns of linguistic minorities have gained an increasingly prominent position on the political agenda of many Western democracies. Consequently, we have seen a substantial growth in efforts to accord recognition and support to languages other than those of the majority (Patten and Kymlicka, 2003). Today, such efforts can be seen in operation in a number of different places across the world and, in particular, in minority nations, such as Quebec (Bourhis, 2001; Chevrier, 2003), Catalonia (Strubell, 1998; McRoberts, 2001; Costa, 2003), the Basque Country (Azurmendi *et al.*, 2001) and Wales (Williams, 2000; 2007). Moreover, the steps taken as part of such efforts have gradually grown more far-reaching in their scope. Indeed, it is now common for policies aimed at promoting the prospects of minority languages to influence numerous aspects of the workings of the modern democratic state, including the justice system, the education system, the media and also the economy.

Significantly, the arguments presented by linguistic minorities as they have sought to demand that the state accords them with greater recognition and support have tended to draw heavily on the language of rights. Most commonly, demands that the state make it possible for the minority language to be used when accessing key public services (e.g. schools, hospitals and social services) or when conducting public business (e.g. in the legislature, the courts or when dealing with public officials) have been justified on the grounds that the speakers of these languages have a right to expect such provisions (Patten, 2009: 103). Nevertheless, it is not only in relation to claims regarding the day-to-day use of a language in key public domains where the vocabulary of rights has been deployed. In several cases, more far-reaching claims that relate to the long-term prospects of the language have also been framed as matters of rights. For example, many minority language activists have insisted that they not only have a right to use their mother tongue as they perform various daily tasks, but that they also have a right to see it survive into the future—a right to know that the language will not disappear, but rather that it will continue to be transferred from generation to generation and used by a community of people as their normal medium of communication.[1]

These various rights claims raise important normative questions. Yet, despite this, their implication for contemporary theories of justice is an issue that, traditionally, has received relatively little attention by normative political theorists. As the prominent Canadian political theorist, Will Kymlicka, observed during the mid-1990s:

> Political theorists have had a lot to say about the language of politics—that is the symbols, metaphors and rhetorical devices of political discourse—but have had virtually nothing to say about the politics of language—that is, decisions about which languages to use in political, legal and educational forums. (Kymlicka, 1995: 2)[2]

However, this seems to be changing, because over the past few years we have seen the emergence of a new body of normative literature which focuses specifically on the issue of language rights.[3] This literature considers a range of relevant questions. Should languages be considered as goods that can give rise to rights? If so, what kinds of rights and what is their status? Who within the political community should be able to claim various linguistic provisions as a matter of right? Should we, for example, distinguish between the linguistic claims presented by national or autochthonous minorities and those presented by immigrant minorities? Moreover, should the language rights that are established be treated as portable ones that can be asserted across the whole of the state or rather tied to particular regional territories?[4]

This paper will seek to contribute to this ongoing debate by focusing in detail on the issue of linguistic survival. It will consider to what extent the members of a language community can demand that they have a right to see their language survive into the future. This question will be considered from two distinct perspectives. First, from an individualist perspective: can the members, as individuals, demand that they have a right to see their language survive? Secondly, from a group perspective: can the members, together as a group, demand that they have a right to see their language survive? In both instances it will be demonstrated that the concept of survival raises a number of substantial normative and ontological problems; ones that mean that a right to such a good would be extremely difficult to justify.[5]

Rights

Before the paper goes on to engage in detail with the questions outlined above, it is necessary to make two important clarifying observations. First, it should be emphasized that it is rights in the moral sense that will be under discussion here, rather than rights in the legal sense. The two are distinct concepts. Legal rights (or positive rights as they are sometimes described) are those which are conceded and enforced by the law. Thus, one can find out what our legal rights are by reading the laws which have been enacted by his/her government, looking up law books, or going to court and asking a judge (Cranston, 1973: 5–6). Moral rights, however, are slightly different. They are not rights that come into existence through the adoption of a particular law or constitutional clause. Rather they are rights that exist independently of such things. They are rights that are based on general moral considerations, such as justice, fairness and equality.

Of course, in practice, these two forms of rights overlap quite often. After all, many of the rights that are conceded and enforced by the law of various societies are rights that happen to reflect and respect certain moral considerations. As Mahoney (2007: 72) observes, "[moral rights] may often be the basis or reason for a new law and a new legal right being introduced in a particular society". However, this overlap does not occur as a matter of course. It is important to bear in mind that in order to respect and maintain certain moral rights it is not essential for the state to give them expression as legal rights. It is entirely possible that a government may be able to adopt a settled policy that secures and respects a particular moral right without resorting to the prodding of legal rights (Patten, 2009: 103). Moreover, every legal right does not necessarily emanate from a more foundational moral right. Certain legal rights are established for instrumental reasons, without recourse to moral arguments and, as a result, rescinding such rights would not cause a grave injustice (Green, 1987: 647).

Secondly, given the focus of this paper on moral rights, it needs to set out its understanding of the particular conditions that need to be met in order to give rise to such rights. On this point this article defers to the prominent legal and political theorist, Joseph Raz (1984; 1986: 166) who, as part of his general interest theory of rights, argues as follows: "X has a right if and only if X can have rights, and other things being equal, an aspect of X's well-being (his interest) is a sufficient reason for holding some other person(s) to be under a duty".

Clearly, therefore, a moral right to a particular good or opportunity is not something that can be accorded lightly. Rather, before such a step can be taken, a series of important conditions must be met. First, the claimant must be an entity that has the capacity to hold a right. In order to possess this most basic capacity the claimant must be an entity to which moral significance can be ascribed. As Peter Jones (1999a: 362) explains, this means that the claimant must be "the sort of thing to which duties can be owed by others and which is capable of being wronged". Secondly, the claimant must possess a need or interest that would be served by establishing the right in question. In other words, the claimant must be able to demonstrate how its well-being would be promoted by according it the right. Thirdly, since according a right to certain actors entails placing duties on others (duties to respect the right and to refrain from undermining it), the need or interest that would be served by establishing the right must be of such significance as to justify the accompanying duties. Or, to adopt the terminology of Ronald Dworkin (1977), the interest must be significant enough to "trump" other considerations.

Survival as an Individual Right

There is a general agreement among political and legal theorists that individual persons are entities that have the capacity to hold rights. Individuals can suffer harm and, given this, they are entities to which moral significance should be ascribed. As a result, it is fitting that an effort to assess whether a right to linguistic survival can be endorsed begins by considering such a right from an individualist perspective. Can the members of a language community, as individuals, demand that they have a right to see their language survive?

An individual right is defined as a right that is held and can be utilized by the individual, independently of others. Moreover, and more importantly, the benefit that would accrue to the individual on his or her own is recognized as a sufficient reason for according the right and establishing the related duties. As Denise Réaume (1994: 120) explains:

> For an individual to claim a right it must be the case that her well-being is sufficient reason to hold others under certain duties. It must be for her sake that the duty is imposed in the sense that only the good to her need be considered.

An example of a right that clearly falls into this category is the right not to be tortured. This is a right that is held and can also be utilized by every individual independently. Moreover, the individual's well-being, on its own, is viewed as a sufficient reason for according such a right. For example, if there was a group of ten people and nine of them claimed that they would take a great deal of pleasure from being able to torture the tenth, few of us would be of the opinion that this was a legitimate reason for allowing them to go ahead. Rather, it is supposed that the interest that the tenth has in not being tortured—in other words, the degree to which his/her well-being would be served should he be left alone—is a sufficient reason for according him a right to such a good and placing a duty on the other nine to refrain. As Green (1987: 649) explains, in such a case "the individual's interest alone, taken by itself, is powerful enough to warrant holding many other people to be under duties".

Therefore, from the above, it is possible to conclude that an individual right to linguistic survival would be a right that was held and could also be utilized by every individual member of the language community, independently of others. Moreover, the linguistic well-being of an individual member, taken by itself, would be seen as a sufficient reason for according such a right and establishing the related duties. To what extent would it be possible to justify such a right? To say the least, the case in favour is a flimsy one.

First, let us consider the moral implications of establishing such a right. It would mean that X, as an individual Xish speaker, would be able to declare that his/her fellow Xish speakers, regardless of their own personal views, have a duty to take all the necessary steps in order to ensure that the Xish language survives into the future. Indeed, even if no other Xish speaker shared this desire, the existence of the individual right would allow him/her to insist that they comply with his/her wishes. Now, to what extent could X argue that he/she possesses needs or interests that are significant enough to justify such a state of affairs? It would be possible for X to argue that the Xish language is fundamental to his/her personal identity and self-understanding—that it is his/her mother tongue, the language with which he/she can communicate and express him/herself with the greatest ease. Furthermore, he/she could argue that being able to live in a society where the Xish language continues to be seen and heard would be a source of great pride. Without doubt, these are not arguments that should be dismissed out of hand. As the prominent political theorist from Québec, Charles Taylor (1994: 25), has argued, people can suffer serious psychological harm if elements of their identity are not acknowledged and treated with respect:

> A person or group of people can suffer real damage, real distortion, if the people or society around them mirror back to them a confining or demeaning or contemptible picture of themselves. Nonrecognition or misrecognition can inflict harm, can be a form of oppression, imprisoning someone in a false, distorted, and reduced mode of being.

However, it is extremely doubtful if even Taylor would wish to treat this potential harm as one that is serious enough to justify the kind of duties that would accompany the establishment of an individual right to linguistic survival. After all, such a right would allow X to tie his/her fellow Xish speakers to a particular linguistic and cultural path, regardless of their own personal views and aspirations. The harm in question is simply not one that can be placed on such a high moral plane.

Yet, even if the substantial moral problems outlined above were ignored, maintaining an argument in favour of according an individual right to linguistic survival would be extremely difficult, if not impossible. This stems from the fact that the concept would also be extremely problematic from an ontological perspective. As Réaume (1988: 7–13) explains, in addition to being a right that is established on the basis of the benefit or well-being that would accrue to the individual on his/her or her own, an individual right is a form of right that can exist only in relation to goods or opportunities that the individual can enjoy independently. The goods or opportunities that are guaranteed by an individual right cannot be ones where the enjoyment is dependant on the co-operation of others.[6]

As far as one can see, it is not an "individualizable good" (Réaume, 1988: 8) of the kind described above that is sought by those who claim a right to linguistic survival. They do not seek a right that will ensure that their language survives in any form possible: for example, that written evidence of the language is preserved so that linguists or historians from the future can study it. Rather, something more specific is sought: a right that will help to ensure that the language continues to be transferred from generation to generation and used by a community of people as their normal medium of communication. Inevitably, in order for such a good to be ensured and then enjoyed, a substantial amount of collaboration between a number of people will be called for. As a result, the good that is sought by those who seek a right to linguistic survival is not one that can be individualized. Rather, it belongs to that class of goods that is described by Réaume (1988: 9) as "participatory goods"—goods that are beyond the scope of individual rights, since they cannot be enjoyed without the co-operation of others.

Therefore, due to a mixture of moral and ontological reasons, it is not possible to argue that members of language communities, as individuals, can hold a right to linguistic survival. Given this, during the next section it will be considered whether such a right can be justified from a group perspective: can the members of a language community, together as a group, demand that they have a right to see their language survive?

Survival as a Group Right

The concept of a group right is not an easy one to discuss as it can be applied in a range of different contexts. Moreover, it is a concept that often generates controversy (Kymlicka, 1994). Nevertheless, at the most general level, a group right can be defined as follows: a right that is held by a group as a group, rather than by its members individually. As Peter Jones (1999a: 354) explains:

> A right is a group right only if it is a right held by a group rather than by its members severally. If rights are held by individuals separately, their shared rights do not add up to a group right even though their rights relate to a characteristic which marks them off, sociologically, as a group. A right is a group right only if it is a right held by a group qua group.[7]

Therefore, to what extent can the members of a language community claim that they have a group right to see their language survive into the future?

Group Rights: The Corporate Conception

As has already been explained, before a right can be accorded it is necessary to establish that the claimant is an entity to which moral significance can be ascribed—that the entity in question is one that can be harmed and to which duties can be owed by others. Given this, many of the early proponents of group rights assumed that their legitimization depended on being able to demonstrate that a particular group—for example a particular nation or cultural community—could possess such moral standing in its own right, independently of its individual members. To quote Jones (2008) once again: "[it was assumed] that ascribing a right to a group entails conceiving the group as a moral entity in its own right: the group must possess a moral standing that is not reducible to the standing of its members".

One prominent political theorist who adopted such reasoning was Vernon Van Dyke (1977; 1982). According to Van Dyke (1982: 24), nations or cultural communities can be conceived as corporate entities that exist and possess an identity that is independent from that of their individual members. Given this, it is possible for such groups to possess interests and suffer wrongs in their own right—interests and wrongs that are not simply the aggregate of those held or suffered by their members severally. As a result, moral standing should be ascribed to such groups and, if they are able to point to sufficiently significant needs or interests, they should be accorded rights, and duties should be placed on others, exactly as would happen in the case of individuals. Indeed, according to this corporate conception, "we might think of a group right as a right of a 'group-individual'" (Jones, 2008).[8] Therefore, to what extent can this traditional conception of a group right be used as a basis for an argument that would legitimize a right to linguistic survival?

One can raise some doubts on the merits of the corporate conception in this case and, once again, the reasons can be both moral and ontological. First, to what extent does it really make sense, ontologically, to view a language community—the relevant group in this case—as one that possesses moral standing in its own right? This may be a perfectly reasonable assumption to make in the case of certain group entities—take, for example, a large corporation. Such an entity can hold interests and duties that are not necessarily reducible to those of the individuals associated with it. As Jones (2008) explains:

> If the Gulf Oil Corporation buys or sells property, or joins a cartel, or is found causally responsible for environmental pollution and held morally responsible for cleaning it up, the Corporation as agent and patient is not reducible to the individuals who are currently associated with it.

However, it is striking to observe that it would be rather difficult to conduct a coherent and intelligible discussion regarding the well-being of the Basque, Catalan or Welsh language communities (or indeed any other language community), which is a step removed from, and that does not engage with, the views and desires of the individuals who speak these languages. Such group entities cannot really suffer harm or bear duties independently of their members. Indeed, the paper's argument here is given added weight by the fact that several recent sociological and socio-linguistic studies have argued strongly against adopting an ontological standpoint that conceptualizes language communities in such a manner, mainly due to the fact that it leads to what is described as "the reification of language" (Nelde *et al.*, 1996; Williams and Morris, 2000).

However, even if some wished to disagree with aspects of this analysis, there remains a serious moral problem that must be faced if one wishes to use the corporate conception as the basis for an argument in favour of a group right to linguistic survival. Since this conception calls on us to view the group as an entity that holds moral significance independently of its members severally, it is the group *qua* group that would also hold any rights that would be established. Therefore, in the case of linguistic survival it would be the language community, independently of its members, that would hold the right. In other words, it would be its right (i.e. the group's right) rather than their right (i.e. the members' right).

Why would this be dangerous from a moral point of view? Quite simply, it would create a situation where the community holds a right against its members and could therefore legitimately place far-reaching linguistic duties on their shoulders. This, in turn, could open the door to a range of morally problematic measures. First, family speech patterns could be monitored and legislation could be introduced that made it illegal for parents who spoke the target language not to transfer it to their children. In addition, legislation could be introduced that made it compulsory for members of the target language community to raise large families in order to increase the number of target language speakers. If such measures did not prove to be sufficient, individuals who spoke the target language could be forced to settle together in a particular location and then prevented from leaving, thus ensuring that there remains one area where a high density of speakers can be found.

Of course, it is not necessary to conclude that such measures are essential in order to guarantee the survival of a particular language, even a minority one. Nevertheless, it is important to understand that adhering to the corporate conception of a group right would entail adopting a moral framework that provides them with at least a *prima facie* justification. If the community has a right to see its traditional language survive into the future, then its members have a moral duty to take all necessary steps in order to guarantee that right (Réaume, 1991: 44). Therefore, any effort to defend a right to linguistic survival that was based on the corporate conception of a group right would be one that stood on shaky ground, both ontologically and morally and, as a result, would be extremely difficult to endorse.

Group Rights: The Collective Conception

The corporate conception is not the only one on which a group right can be based. An alternative approach, based on the collective conception, is also possible. This more recent conception of a group right was introduced originally by Joseph Raz (1986: 207–209; see also Margalit and Raz, 1990) and, unsurprisingly, it builds on aspects of his general interest theory of rights. According to Raz (1986: 208), a group should be accorded a right as a group to a particular good or opportunity if it meets the following conditions:

> First [the right] exists because an aspect of the interest of human beings justifies holding some person(s) to be subject to a duty. Second, the interests in question are the interests of individuals as members of a group in a public good and the right is a right to that public good because it serves their interest as members

of the group. Thirdly, the interest of no single member of that group in that public good is sufficient by itself to justify holding another person to be subject to a duty.

Therefore, a group should be accorded a right as a group if its members severally possess a shared need or interest that is significant enough to justify the necessary duties, and if the need or interest of any individual member, taken on its own, is not deemed sufficient to justify those same duties.

Thus, there is an important difference between this conception of a group right and the corporate conception discussed above. The collective conception does not require us to treat the group as an entity that holds moral standing independently of its individual members. As Peter Jones (2008) explains:

> ... a group right conceived in this way does not entail giving moral status to the group *qua* group that is separate from that of its members severally. Rather, the moral standing that underwrites the group right is the moral standing of the several individuals who jointly hold the right. The group right is therefore conceived as "their" right rather than "its' right".

Yet, given that it is the moral standing of the group's individual members that grounds the right, to what extent can one say that it is really a group right? Indeed, at first glance it appears to resemble an individual right. However, this would be a misguided conclusion. A right that was established under the auspices of the collective conception would be one that an individual could not hold on his or her own. Rather, due to the fact that the need or interest that gives rise to the right is a collective one, which an individual must share with others, it is a right that can be held only by a group of people together. To quote Jones (2008) once more:

> In this conception, a group right is still properly so-called because the individuals who make up the right-holding group possess a right together that none of them possess separately. The right is not a mere aggregation of rights held individually by the members of the group.

To what extent can this alternative conception be applied to the current discussion regarding linguistic survival and be used as the basis for an argument in favour of acknowledging such a right?

The ontological and moral problems identified in relation to the corporate conception do not arise in relation to the collective conception. First, the collective conception does not call on us to treat the group as an entity that holds moral significance independently of its members. Rather, it is the individual group members and the needs or interests that they hold together that is treated as significant. Secondly, and largely as a result of this, the collective conception does not lead to a state of affairs where the group holds a right against its own members and can place them under significant duties. Rather, it is the group members that hold the right according to this conception. Therefore, it is those members together who decide whether the right will be utilized or, more importantly, whether it will not. Given this, can one conclude that a right to linguistic survival that is based on the collective conception should be accorded?

Significant problems remain. Imagine that the current generation of Xish speakers follow Raz's guidelines: that they succeed in demonstrating that they possess shared needs or interests in relation to the Xish language and that these are significant enough to generate a right to see it survive into the future. Should such a right be accorded, what kind of duties would need to be established and who would be expected to bear them? Among other things, since the right that is being sought is one that seeks to ensure the maintenance of a particular good over time, according a right to linguistic survival would, in this case, involve placing future Xish speakers under substantial duties. After all, in order to ensure the right, generation after generation of Xish speakers would be expected, regardless of their own personal opinions, to continue to use the language as their normal medium of communication and to transfer it to their children. Should this not happen, the language would not survive in any meaningful sense and, as a result, the right of the current generation would be undermined.

To what extent can such a move be justified? As part of recent discussions regarding historical injustice a number of political theorists have come to the conclusion that it is possible, in certain circumstances, for one generation to place duties on the shoulders of its descendants (see, for example, Thompson, 2002). However, there is a significant difference between the kind of duties envisioned in these discussions and the kind under consideration here. The transgenerational duties referred to in the historical injustice literature are ones owed to the members of other groups—duties to continue to treat the members of those groups with respect or to take steps to alleviate the effects of past wrongs—and not ones where the members of one generation are duty bound to stick rigidly to a cultural and linguistic path that was set for them by their predecessors. This second form of transgenerational duty would be problematic, as it would require the adoption of a point of view that does not allow various generations to have the opportunity to interpret their cultural inheritance on their own terms and to evaluate and adapt aspects of it according to their priorities. Perhaps some would be happy enough to curtail such opportunities for the sake of cultural or linguistic continuity. However, for those who adhere to a political morality that places at least some emphasis on individual autonomy, it would represent a step too far (Kymlicka, 1995). As a result, even when approached from the perspective of the collective conception of a group right—a conception that is generally acknowledged as being less restrictive than its corporate counterpart—a right to linguistic survival would remain extremely difficult to justify.

Conclusion

This paper has drawn upon the work of a number of contemporary political theorists in order to assess whether the members of a language community can demand that they have a right to see their language survive into the future. First, the issue was discussed from an individualist perspective. Following that it was considered from a group perspective, with consideration being given to both the corporate and collective conceptions of a group right. In every case it was demonstrated that the concept of survival raises a number of substantial ontological and moral problems and, as a result, a right to such a good would be extremely difficult to justify.[9]

What are the implications of such a conclusion? It should be emphasized that the argument advanced in this paper does not in any way suggest that it is unacceptable for a state to take steps to promote the prospects of a minority language. Moreover, it would not be unacceptable for these steps to include measures that do, in fact, facilitate the survival of that language into the future. However, what would prove to be extremely problematic would be declaring that this long-term survival was something that had to be ensured *as a matter of right*—that it was imperative from a moral point of view that the language did not disappear, but rather that it continue to be transferred from generation to generation and used by a community of people as their normal medium of communication. Therefore, it is not suggested that minority language activists are misguided in their efforts to ensure that the state accords their tongues with a greater degree of recognition and support. Rather, what is claimed is that those efforts are undermined, not strengthened, by being based on arguments that claim the existence of a fundamental right to linguistic survival. As a result, those activists who have tended to frame their linguistic claims in such terms need to reflect critically on their arguments and develop a new conceptual vocabulary.

Notes

[1]For examples of such claims in relation to the Welsh language, see Welsh Language Society (2005) and Brooks (2009). For discussions of linguistic survival in the Canadian context, see Brett (1991: 347), Green (1987: 639) and Taylor (1994: 40).

[2]This observation by Kymlicka was based on comments that were originally made by Brian Weinstein (1983).

[3]See, for example, Carens (2000), May (2001) and Patten (2001; 2003a; 2003b; 2009); see also the various contributions to Kymlicka and Patten (2003).

[4]For a comprehensive review of the normative literature on language policy and language rights, see Patten and Kymlicka (2003).

[5]On the issue of what constitutes a language and, more importantly, what distinguishes a language from a dialect, the paper will proceed on the basis of an acknowledgement of the increasingly accepted view that a consideration of purely linguistic factors is not sufficient; a mixture of social, cultural, political, and historical factors also needs to be considered (see Chambers and Trudgill, 1980).

[6]It should be noted that it is the enjoyment of the good or opportunity that is of importance, according to Réaume (1988: 8), and not the more fundamental process of its production. She explains that the need for co-operation with regards to production does not necessarily lead to a similar situation with regards to enjoyment. She refers, for example, to the case of clean air. This is an important good that can be produced only if a group of people collaborate with each other and refrain from emitting pollution. However, an individual can take advantage of and enjoy clean air on his or her own and, given this, Réaume insists that it is possible to hold an individual right to clean air.

[7]Peter Jones is a scholar who has written extensively on the issue of group rights (see Jones 1999a; 1999b; 2008; 2009) and his ideas proved particularly influential in this section of the paper.

[8]A number of other scholars have also adopted the corporate conception as a basis for their deliberations regarding the merits of group rights. See, for example, McDonald (1991), Addis (1992) and Narveson (1991).

[9]It should be noted that the particular territorial context within which the language community found itself would not have any bearing on this conclusion. The problems identified as ones that arise in relation to claims regarding the right to linguistic survival (whether in its individualistic, corporate or collective forms) would be as relevant regardless of whether the language community happened

to be one that was territorially concentrated or territorially dispersed. I am grateful to the anonymous reviewer for pressing me to make this point.

References

Addis, A. (1992), Individualism, Communitarianism and the Rights of Ethnic Minorities, *Notre Dame Law Review*, Vol.67, No.3, pp.615–667.

Azurmendi, M.-J., Bachoc, E. and Zabaleta, F. (2001), Reversing Language Shift: The Case of Basque, in J.A. Fishman (ed.), *Can Threatened Languages be Saved?* Clevedon: Multilingual Maters.

Bourhis, R. Y. (2001), Reversing Language Shift in Quebec, in J.A. Fishman (ed.), *Can Threatened Languages be Saved?* Clevedon: Multilingual Matters.

Brett, N. (1991), Language Laws and Collective Rights, *Canadian Journal of Law and Jurisprudence*, Vol.4, No.2, pp.347–360.

Brooks, S. (2009), *Yr Hawl i Oroesi: Ysgrifau Gwleidyddol a Diwylliannol*. Llanrwst: Gwasg Carreg Gwalch.

Carens, J. H. (2000), *Culture, Citizenship and Community: A Contextual Exploration of Justice as Evenhandedness*. Oxford: Oxford University Press.

Chambers, J. and Trudgill, P. (1980), *Dialectology*. Cambridge: Cambridge University Press.

Chevrier, M. (2003), A Language Policy for a Language in Exile, in P. Larrivée (ed.), *Linguistic Conflict and Language Laws: Understanding the Quebec Case*. London: Palgrave Macmillan.

Costa, J. (2003), Catalan Linguistic Policy: Liberal or Illiberal? *Nations and Nationalism*, Vol.9, No.3, pp.413–432.

Cranston, M. (1973), *What are Human Rights?* London: The Bodley Head.

Dworkin, R. (1977), *Taking Rights Seriously*. London: Duckworth.

Green, L. (1987), Are Language Rights Fundamental? *Osgoode Hall Law Journal*, Vol.25, pp.639–669.

Jenkins, G. H. (1999), Wales, the Welsh and the Welsh Language: Introduction, in G.H. Jenkins (ed.), *The Welsh Language and its Social Domains 1801–1911*. Cardiff: University of Wales Press.

Jenkins, G. H. and Williams, M. A. (2000), The Fortunes of the Welsh Language 1900–2000: Introduction, in G. JenkinsH. and M.A. Williams (eds), *Let's Do Our Best for the Ancient Tongue: The Welsh Language in the Twentieth Century*. Cardiff: University of Wales Press.

Jones, P. (1999a), Group Rights and Group Oppression, *The Journal of Political Philosophy*, Vol.7, No.4, pp.353–377.

Jones, P. (1999b), Human Rights, Group Rights and People's Rights, *Human Rights Quarterly*, Vol.21, No.1, pp.80–107.

Jones, P. (2008), Group Rights, *The Stanford Encyclopaedia of Philosophy*, Available at http://plato.stanford.edu/entries/rights-group/ (accessed 10 December 2012).

Jones, P. (ed.). (2009), *Group Rights*. Aldershot: Ashgate.

Kymlicka, W. (1994), Individual and Group Rights, in J. Baker (ed.), *Group Rights*. Toronto: University of Toronto Press.

Kymlicka, W. (1995), *Multicultural Citizenship*. Oxford: Oxford University Press.

Kymlicka, W. and Patten, A. (eds) (2003), *Language Rights and Political Theory*. Oxford: Oxford University Press.

Mahoney, J. (2007), *The Challenge of Human Rights*. Oxford: Blackwell Publishing.

Margalit, A. and Raz, J. (1990), National Self-determination, *Journal of Philosophy*, Vol.87, No.9, pp.439–461.

May, S. (2001), *Language and Minority Rights: Ethnicity, Nationalism and the Politics of Language*. London: Longman.

McDonald, M. (1991), Should Communities Have Rights? Reflections on Liberal Individualism, *Canadian Journal of Law and Jurisprudence*, Vol.4, No.2, pp.217–237.

McRoberts, K. (2001), *Catalonia: Nation Building Without a State*. Oxford: Oxford University Press.

Narveson, J. (1991), Collective Rights, *Canadian Journal of Law and Jurisprudence*, Vol.4, No.2, pp.329–345.

Nelde, P., Strubell, M. and Williams, G. (1996), *Euromosaic: The Production and Reproduction of the Minority Language Groups in the European Union*. Luxembourg: Office for Official Publications of the European Communities.

Patten, A. (2001), Political Theory and Language Policy, *Political Theory*, Vol.29, No.5, pp.683–707.

Patten, A. (2003a), Liberal Neutrality and Language Policy, *Philosophy and Public Affairs*, Vol.31, No.4, pp.356–386.

Patten, A. (2003b), What Kind of Bilingualism?, in W. Kymlicka and A. Patten (eds), *Language Rights and Political Theory*. Oxford: Oxford University Press.

Patten, A. (2009), The Justification of Minority Language Rights, *The Journal of Political Philosophy*, Vol.17, No.1, pp.102–128.

Patten, A. and Kymlicka, W. (2003), Introduction: Language Rights and Political Theory: Context, Issues and Approaches, in W. Kymlicka and A. Patten (eds), *Language Rights and Political Theory*. Oxford: Oxford University Press.

Raz, J. (1984), On the Nature of Rights, *Mind*, Vol.93, pp.194–214.

Raz, J. (1986), *The Morality of Freedom*. Oxford: Clarendon Press.

Réaume, D. (1988), Individuals, Groups and Rights to Collective Goods, *University of Toronto Law Journal*, Vol.38, No.1, pp.1–27.

Réaume, D. (1991), The Constitutional Protection of Language: Security or Survival?, in D. Schneiderman (ed.), *Language and the State: The Law and Politics of Identity*. Cowansville: Éditions Yvon Blais.

Réaume, D. (1994), The Group Right to Linguistic Security: Whose Right, What Duties?, in J. Baker (ed.), *Group Rights*. Toronto: University of Toronto Press.

Strubell, M. (1998), Language, Democracy and Devolution in Catalonia, *Current Issues in Language and Society*, Vol.5, No.3, pp.146–180.

Taylor, C. (1994), The Politics of Recognition, in A. Gutmann (ed.), *Multiculturalism and the Politics of Recognition*. Princeton: Princeton University Press.

Thompson, J. (2002), *Taking Responsibility for the Past*. Cambridge: Polity Press.

Van Dyke, V. (1977), The Individual, the State and Ethnic Communities in Political Theory, *World Politics*, Vol.29, No.3, pp.343–369.

Van Dyke, V. (1982), Collective Entities and Moral Rights: Problems in Liberal-Democratic Thought, *Journal of Politics*, Vol.44, No.1, pp.21–40.

Weinstein, B. (1983), *The Civic Tongue: Political Consequences of Language Choices*. London: Longman.

Welsh Language Society (2005), *A New Welsh Language Act: A Real Opportunity*. Aberystwyth: Welsh Language Society.

Williams, C. H. (2000), On Recognition, Resolution and Revitalization, in C. H. Williams (ed.), *Language Revitalization: Policy and Planning in Wales*. Cardiff: University of Wales Press.

Williams, C. H. (2007), Articulating the Horizons of Welsh, in C.H. Williams (ed.), *Language and Governance*. Cardiff: University of Wales Press.

Williams, G. and Morris, D. (2000), *Language Planning and Language Use: Welsh in a Global Age*. Cardiff: University of Wales Press.

Perfidious Hope: The Legislative Turn in Official Minority Language Regimes

COLIN HASLEHURST WILLIAMS

School of Welsh, Cardiff University, Cardiff UK

ABSTRACT Minority language transmission is no longer based solely on family, associated networks and statutory education but is increasingly influenced by the so-called 'legislative turn'. This paper focuses on some of the side-effects of this latter trend as they appear in two of the most advanced cases in that field (the Basque Country and Ireland). The aim is to identify the reach and significance of the appeal to law and to anticipate some of the more challenging aspects for official language policy in terms of professionalization, juridical relationship between the minority and the majority and between the individual citizen, the language community and the state.

Introduction

Historically minority language promotion has as its fundamental base the transmission of the language in the home, the community and associated group networks, agencies and institutions. In many European contexts these pillars of language production and reproduction appear to be weakening and, in consequence, a great deal of collective energy has been focused on navigating minority interests into the mainstream of statutory education, local government, the media and representative political assemblies. Hopes are pinned on the growth in numbers of new speakers, produced by a reformed education system, which is conceived as a bulwark against the continuing decline of native or first-language speakers within their historical heartlands.

Allied to this promotional and interventionist activity generated by official language strategies there has been a recognition that unless the rights of individuals and communities to be free to speak their own chosen language in the widest possible domains is recognized in law, then the potential to speak a minority language would always be limited by the weight of the prevailing hegemonic language. In consequence a great deal of attention has been paid to securing minimum rights for minority languages in a raft of new laws at European, state and sub-state level—what we may term the legislative turn. Despite this legislative turn, the struggle in and over contending languages in the modern state is far more than a question of socio-legal recognition and rights. For many, the language struggle is a matter of survival itself and can constitute the single most important reason for being active within politics and democratic representation. For others, historical injustices can only be exposed and articulated through sustained violence against the state so as to draw attention to the perceived structured inequalities which obtain within polities.

Consequently language-related issues in modern polities can appear divisive, idiosyncratic and even mysterious, because unlike health-care provision, taxation or public order arrangements, they do not appear to be universal, but rather partial and factional. Within liberal democracies the growth of an increasingly plural and diverse citizenship has been accompanied by claims and counter-claims that the prevailing rules of engagement for many groups are both discriminatory and unjust. Language activists, having spent a generation constructing an infrastructure which is supportive of minority language promotion in education, the media and local government, are now engaged in specifying in law, just what are the duties of national government to engage with citizens in the language of their choice by specifying the obligations of local authorities and public bodies to deliver bilingual or language-specific services. When such duties appear to be abrogated, then an appeal to law, to natural justice, to specific rights becomes far more prevalent and this trend shows no sign of abating. Citizens and civil society organizations are becoming more articulate, and more conscious of the inner workings of government and public administration, so that they now frame their demands according to professional standards underpinned by evidence-based arguments. In effect they become shadow language policy and planning advisers, well able to match the government rhetoric and capable of drafting quite complex pieces of legislation as a template for official imitation.[1] Thus, we are entering new territory as regards official language strategy where both promotion and regulation form important parts of policy implementation at all levels in the political hierarchy.

A number of factors influence the scope and duration of language policy. The most critical is the role which an ever-changing party political context has on the formulation, implementation, revision and sometimes weakening of official language strategies. The second is the relationship between political representatives, senior civil servants and engaged interest groups drawn from within civil society. The third is the role which legislative reform, court challenges and remedies and judicial review play in the process of protecting or modifying language strategies.

Cairney (2012: 33) has identified the following stages, which can act as a conceptual and professional framework for further analysis, as follows:

- *Agenda setting.* Identifying problems that require government attention, deciding which issues deserve the most attention and defining the nature of the problem.
- *Policy formulation.* Setting objectives, identifying the cost and estimating the effect of solutions, choosing from a list of solutions and selecting policy instruments.
- *Legitimation.* Ensuring that the chosen policy instruments have support. It can involve one or a combination of legislative approval, executive approval, seeking consent through consultation with interest groups and referends.
- *Implementation.* Establishing or employing an organization to take responsibility for implementation, ensuring that the organization has the resources (such as staffing,

money and legal authority) to do so, and making sure that policy decisions are carried out as planned.

- *Evaluation.* Assessing the extent to which the policy was successful or the policy decision was the correct one; was it implemented correctly and, if so, had the desired effect?
- *Policy maintenance, succession and termination.* Considering if the policy should be continued, modified or discontinued.

This paper is concerned with the implementation aspects of policy. In particular it asks how are language policies implemented in the face of legal, political obstacles, especially where there are multiple jurisdictions and where they must be implemented by officials, who may not be reticent to operate the full potential of the designated policy. Cairney's description suggests a rational and synoptic process, but, in the cases we will be examining, there is abundant evidence of idiosyncratic and reluctant behaviour. Thus, the legal framework allows a degree of certainty of policy potential, but it does not necessarily guarantee the desired policy outcomes, hence the conundrum of analysing a perfidious hope.

The Legislative Turn

A major influence on the legislative turn has been the development of European Human Rights law. The European Convention on Human Rights (1953–99), together with the decisions of the European Court of Human Rights (ECtHR), has been illustrated superbly in Janis *et al.* (2008). The promise of freedom from discrimination and freedom to extend the target language to new domains, such as health care and education, has ushered in a new era of enabling and empowering rights. Given the diversity of the legal systems in Europe the effect in national law of the European Convention on Human Rights is rarely immediate and often diffuse. However, the symbolic weight of recourse to such conventions is profound for historically disadvantaged minorities. The principle of non-discrimination in international law includes both the direct discrimination related to race, religion, language, ethnicity and national origins and indirect discrimination. Having been reluctant to accord some degree to salience to indirect discrimination for much of its history, the ECtHR has signalled a shift in emphasis by recognizing that a combination of the above discriminatory elements can be citable. A good recent example is the Czech Republic's policy of placing Roma pupils in special schools when they failed to achieve a minimum score on an intelligence test which the ECtHR judged was a case of indirect discrimination (Ahmed, 2011: 30).[2] Under international law norms, states are liable for their own breaches and for failure to prevent breaches. Equally telling is the notion that human rights instruments are now applicable to all persons within a state's jurisdiction, rendering the nationality of the individual irrelevant. There is also an allowance for positive measures to overcome structural discrimination and, in consequence, one would anticipate that historically disadvantaged indigenous language minorities would have been among the first beneficiaries of this change of emphasis, reach and significance in European law.

Given this, it may seem surprising to concur with Ahmed's (2011: 168) interpretation that there is no right under EU law concerning minority language education or to establish minority language institutions. At first sight this may suggest that the legal framework of the EU remains antagonistic to the development of minority linguistic rights within international law. This is certainly the impression given by many language activists and non-governmental organizations (NGOs). However, on closer examination some of the lacunae in the EU's approach to this aspect of language diversity relate directly to the lack of competence at the EU level to regulate minority linguistic rights. Yet we need to be very careful in downplaying the role of the EU and of other European-wide institutions too readily in determining language policy, or in influencing language rights, for there has been a considerable degree of attention paid both to the political and legal significance of recognizing 'unity in diversity' as an operative principle in key policy areas. The difficulty, of course, is that the diversity under consideration does not always accord with the aims and ambitions of so-called minority or lesser-used language speakers, but rather tends to favour the interests of constituent states. However, with the enlargement of the EU these considerations have been tempered by a growing awareness of the need to reflect the inherent complexity of member states, many of whom are relatively small in demolingusitic terms, such as the Baltic States and Slovenia, and face similar issues of identity preservation, language competition and constructing a framework for the recognition of plural citizenship akin to that undertaken within Catalonia or the Basque Country.[3]

Breziger (2010) has surveyed the contribution which the EU has made to the recognition of minority languages in terms of legislative enactments and key documents. His analysis also focuses on respect for diversity, new basic standards, the rights of persons belonging to minorities, the prohibition of discrimination and the language of treaties. His analysis demonstrates that the biggest failing has been an incomplete understanding of the purchase of EU law and of its inconsistent application in relation to many linguistic minorities and regional minority languages (RML). Beyond the EU there has been a raft of legislative initiatives, as discussed by Dunbar (2007) and Nic Craith (2007), who draw attention to the especial salience of the 1992 Council of Europe's European Charter for Regional or Minority Languages, which came into force in March 1998 in instigating a greater concern with language legislation in Europe.[4] Thus, the legislative turn operates at international, state and regional level and has routinely recognized a range of languages, such as Catalan, Basque, Irish, Welsh, Gaelic and Swedish in Finland, within new, apparently more robust, jurisdictional contexts.

While welcoming this increased recognition, I have a fundamental reservation that in several real-world experiences the inconsistent application of statutory obligations to deliver bilingual services or to exercise minority language rights undermines in practice and, thus, in legal effect the often pristine declarations of linguistic co-equality or constitutionally guaranteed primacy for several official languages.

There is a second legislative turn at work, namely a context-dependent diminution of selected legislative instruments so assiduously won through stealth politics. What is most troubling about this further turn is that it represents the state's failure to honour the constitutionally or parliamentary guaranteed rights and obligations of official minority language speakers. Such trends do not appear as serious a failing as other breaches of established law. In many respects one can well understand why, as it is more often the minority alone which objects to such inconsistent or poor quality public service and, when complaints are made, they are perceived as a minor irrelevance from a dissatisfied section of the citizenry. This raises questions which are addressed by specialists, such as Woeherling (2010), as to whether linguistic rights are best conceived of as fundamental rights or context-dependent rights.

It is in order to regulate such inconsistent behaviour that a number of polities have revised their primary language legislation and established stronger regulatory agencies, including the office of language commissioners, of late. I want to focus on the operation of this second legislative turn in selected jurisdictions so as to identify the reach and significance of the appeal to law and to anticipate some of the more problematic aspects for official language policy of moving from a preoccupation with the promotion of a target language to a preoccupation with the regulation of the target language. I argue that this transition not only bespeaks a more professional and responsible approach to official language implementation, but also influences the political and juridical relationship between the minority and the majority and between the individual citizen, the language community and the state. Each of these has normative consequences for the operation of the state, its sub-state parliaments, policy divergence and electoral behaviour.

Basque Reasons Why Policy Rhetoric is not Fulfilled in Language and Employment Legislation

So many of the recent policies and promotional initiatives practised in the Basque Autonomous Community derive from an ideological and cultural ferment generated over a hundred years ago and more acutely during the period of revitalization, 1927–36. The revivalist movement, which included writers, poets, priests, journalist and teachers, was committed to the idea of revitalizing the Basque language and culture, while nearly all the participants espoused Basque nationalist tendencies.[5] Among the more notable writer activists were Lizeadi, Lamaxeta (both nicknames) and Aitzel who was a priest, the first president of *Euskaltzaindia* and whose formative contribution to language planning was celebrated recently in Bilbao.[6]

The nationalist intelligentsia argued that if Basque were to be used as a language of administration, of law and health care, it first had to be standardized and its vocabulary widened to suit the demands of modern social, economic and political life. Thus, language promotion leading to normalization has been a profound goal since the 1920s and 1930s. In common with similar movements in Catalonia, Ireland and Wales, the initial concern was with societal bilingualism and education rather than legislation.[7] Bilingual education was a central justification for the development of the movement and instituting the establishment of new schools was a notable achievement, which was tolerated because of the precedent set by the *fueros* which allowed a certain degree of autonomy. Regional governance has had the competence to select teachers for public schools since 1857, and certainly since 1878–80, but ongoing debates with Madrid slowed the progress of the expansion of Basque education. In October 1919, *Euskaltzaindia,* the Royal Basque Academy was established and its first aim was to create a unified Basque language. The debate raged for a long time as to whether or not a unified language was needed. At the time there were four literary dialects. The dominant argument used by opponents of unification was that a greater need was to improve the current variant forms so that ordinary people, who in the main had not received a great deal of formal education, could access these forms. "Let us enrich the knowledge of Basque through promoting all varieties rather than subsume them to one unified form" was a common campaign slogan.[8] Others argued that what was needed was a unified language based on the Central Dialect. As President of *Euskaltzaindia*, Aitzel proposed that a comprehensive survey be undertaken to identify which verbs, auxiliaries, case endings and other morphological and syntactical features were still prevalent and where within the territory.[9] Thus, was initiated a Basque concern with mass survey investigations which continued for several years, but came to a stop with the advent of the Civil War, even if the data collected remain in numerous notebooks. This type of mass social survey data gathering was reinstituted after the restoration of democracy and now features as a prominent element in evidence-based language policy.

What is intriguing is just how many achievements and initiatives the early activists brought to reality in the early period in their attempts to give public recognition to the Basque language, to mobilize key international personalities so as to influence the flow of ideas and promote public debate about threatened or subjugated nations in Europe. They also organized competitions and tournaments in Vitoria, Donostia which sought to improve the status of folk customs and popular culture of the day. Such events were held both in rural taverns and in the most prestigious palaces of culture, such as the modern theatre in Donostia. The aim throughout was to give a much higher status to the real, authentic and grounded culture of the Basque people. A second type of initiative was the writing of books for children so that they could learn to read and write, to participate in competitions and to contribute to Basque newspapers. All this came to a halt at the time of the Civil War, where Spanish and not Basque was now used and large numbers abandoned Basque altogether for two generations. After the Civil War, people tried to pick up the pieces of the puzzle, but they did so increasingly outside the ideological framework of the older system. Nevertheless it is remarkable how many of the older ideas and themes still inform official initiatives and motivate those activists who are currently engaged with various aspects of language policy and planning.

Today the Basque language has been institutionalized and normalized. The Consultative Agency on the Basque Language is the principal agency responsible for plans to promote Basque.[10] Inevitably, perhaps, within a field of public policy which is as sensitive and historically riven as is language in Spain and the Basque Autonomous Community, there is an ongoing tension as to what should constitute the main elements of Basque language policy and planning. Thirty years ago, in the run up to the passage of the 1982 language normalization legislation, the nationalists were fully aware of the need to seek a broad consensus and, at that time, the law obtained support from the Spanish Socialist Party, though not from the state-wide centre-right Popular Party. Over the years this consensus had largely come to an end, as the resultant policies began to alter the status quo. The very close relationship between nationalism and language had alienated many within the other parties who tend to view any attempt to promote the language as a surrogate for nationalist empowerment. Consequently some of the near-permanent opposition parties share a history of rejection of pro-Basque language legislation and policies.[11]

Recent strenuous efforts to achieve political agreement, so as to make the Basque autonomous system more effectual and to reduce the appeal of violence, have focused on renewed nationalist attempts to draw in the socialists to this overarching consensus.[12] The socialists, for their part, have recognized their role in this dynamic political culture and have sought to change their image so as to participate more fully in the general discussions. They remain diametrically opposed to the *Partido Nacionalista Vasco* (PNV, Basque Nationalist Party) on economic policy and on the issue of class versus national-based identification Thus, despite socialist support for the strengthening of an official bilingual society, when they came to power in March 2009 (with the support of the conservative *Partido Popular* (PP, People's Party)) many of the previous PNV reforms were put on hold.

Despite this reversal, the PNV-led coalitions up to 2009 had succeeded in establishing a strong statutory underpinning for language policy measures. However, creating the opportunity is one thing, implementing the language reforms is quite another as the process is subject to great variation in interpretation and application by governmental agencies of a lower order (departments of the regional government, provincial (i.e. county) councils, town and village councils) or in Spain by the behaviour of agencies under the control of the state-wide government. No matter how difficult it might appear at the time to pass legislation allowing for Basque to be used in public administration, without a corresponding investment in the supportive infrastructure, such legislation is likely to remain as a token of intent. It is recognized that building capacity so as to implement government plans and schemes so often lags behind the declaration of rights. In consequence we need to assess to what extent the rights are fully honoured by reference to the government's commitment to significant training in language awareness and investment in improving its public servants' language and organizational skills.

The disjuncture between the rhetoric of government policy and the daily workings of Basque public administration is a classic illustration of my title's reference to a perfidious hope. The foundation of Basque language policy is the 1982 Law for the Normalization of the use of Basque by which statute citizens have the right to address any government body in the Basque Government's territory in Basque and to be dealt with in Basque. The law insists that the administration is bound to attend to citizens in the official language of their choice and, where it is unaware of their choice, to provide information in both languages.[13] Given that when the act was passed the administration in the Basque Autonomous Community was not in a position to comply fully with the new law, gradual implementation was planned for in two ways; the first was the language profile scheme and the second was the authority-wide language schemes, called *erabilera-planak*, i.e. plans of language use. I want to examine the degree to which both these instruments have been implemented and with what consequence for the realization of language rights.

Within the language profile scheme all public service posts in regional administration have a number of published requisites, including the level of education required, subject studied, good health, lack of a prison record and other elements. The 1989 Public Service law added two additional requisites to be published in the official gazette(s) along with the others, namely the level of Basque required to carry out the functions associated with that post (at present one of four levels, to be proved by exam) and the date, if any, by which the holder of the post must prove that (s)/he has attained the required level.

The Basque Government has instituted several language schemes. Here I focus on its core scheme involving just over 6000 employees carrying out tasks which derive from internal workings of the civil service.[14] I have argued previously that the scheme was not effective and did not deliver a comprehensive service by which citizens could engage with the administration in the language of their choice (Williams, 2008). The law is perfectly adequate in the present circumstances as it details how the administration must attend people in the official language of choice and, if that choice is unknown, in both official languages. However, its implementation as a social fact is wanting. When reporting on its own implementation results for the 1998–2002 period the government acknowledged that it had not achieved its objectives, as

- the number of posts created does not reach the level of Basque specified,
- the number of posts with a date of compulsion is low as compared to the number of posts which should have such a date,
- the low number of permanent post holders in posts with date of compulsion having certified achievement of required level,
- the low number of administrative units with bilingual status.

Clearly these results do not fully reflect policy objectives.[15] Moreover the system should be measuring the increase in officials' knowledge, and measuring how far citizen demand is being satisfied both orally and in writing. This appears not to be a priority for any agency within government, because the Basque Government has concentrated on increasing knowledge instead of use. That is, it has sought to emphasize policy input at the expense of output or delivery. This is not an isolated case, but one which—we shall see—is repeated in the case of Ireland and reflects quite a common failing within officially bilingual administrative systems.

My field work and interviews suggest that several factors account for this failing. The first is bureaucratization itself, for the whole scheme has spawned an immense amount of regulations and paperwork, forever postponing the time for real action. The obsession with cover-all-contingencies and detailed planning has delayed the introduction of simple, effective, immediately applicable measures.

Secondly, plans have not been made, thus not a single government department actually produced a plan during the formative period 1998–2002 and those that have been drafted subsequently are often far too generic and non-binding. Thus, in spite of all the planning apparatus being in place, including regulations about how to implement agreed plans, the appointment of officials in most departments dedicated full-time to the task, in spite of viability reports in most departments based on data collection, no plan was actually completed and, hence, none implemented. In the meantime, no interim measures were implemented, except the provision of language training for officials and the subsequent exams needed to satisfy the requirements of entry or confirmation within the public sector.

Thirdly, there remains a disjuncture reflecting a conflict of interest within the system as some departments are not really interested in taking the planning on board. In particular, the assignation of dates of compulsion gives rise to conflict as expressed to the representatives of human resources, because this requirement reduces the opportunities for a department to manipulate personnel movements. Thus, conflicts frequently arise between departments wishing to assign a particular date and/or level of Basque to a post and the Sub-department of Language Policy, which oversees the system and checks that departments are conforming to the rules of the game.

Fourthly, the absence of mainstream leadership and buy-in from senior management is a serious issue. It is one thing to focus on the Sub-department of Language Policy's interest in doing things correctly; it is quite another to ask whether the politicians and senior managers in each department are really interested in, or committed to, carrying out government language policy. Lip-service is almost invariably paid to the policy, but in some cases precious little done. In such cases the language planning officials, often in junior positions, have little power to push through the planning agenda and implementation, without proper management backing. As with concurrent developments in Ireland and Wales, the role of middle managers in articulating official language policy is a major determinant of the rate and effectiveness of implementation.

Fifthly, the reticence of civil servants to apply the skills so assiduously garnered and certified through formal examination and testing belies the system's lack of insistence that they utilize such skills in a regular fashion. The fact that an official learns Basque in no way guarantees willingness to use it. Certification is sufficient to improve one's chances of promotion. There is no follow-up to ensure that government-paid language training actually leads to language use: sometimes it does, sometimes not. This lack of consistency and professional accountability, in contrast to what happens in the Canadian federal civil service, is a major weakness of the system and gives the lie as to how essential it is to operate in a bilingual fashion so as to honour the titular rights of the citizens to have a language choice in their dealings with officialdom.

A sixth element is that the system is top-heavy and there has been insufficient attention paid to bottom-up aspects of planning and very few attempts to involve officials in the language planning and implementation process let alone to harness their goodwill, where it exists. The Basque Government's application of its scheme is a classic top-down case of planning, purveyed through specialist language planners. This is related to the generic top-down culture which so characterized the Basque Government during that initial period where modern management methods seemed to be relatively little known.

This weakness is reflective of a widespread misunderstanding of the principal objectives of normalization and planning, for many officials believe that the object of language planning within the Basque Government is merely to ensure that all texts are bilingual. For them Basque is a symbol of a bilingual society rather than a medium of active communication. Consequently it does not really matter what the citizen's language of choice is as they will automatically get a bilingual reply. At face value this appears to be treating both languages on the basis of equality as happens in Ireland and Wales. However, this bilingual practice, insiders believe, is extremely damaging, for if Basque is to survive it must have its own authentic communicative value. If the Spanish text is always alongside in official documentation, the Basque text is likely to lose that value because recipients, unless young, almost invariably find the Spanish text easier to read; and, because as the Basque text is often a mere translation, it is usually less well written and comprehensible. If, on the other hand, a monolingual Basque text were to be provided for a client or a customer at their request, then officers will have to make sure of its comprehensibility before sending it out; the text, moreover, becomes communicative, rather than merely symbolic.

While this aspect of information diffusion has improved in recent years, given the great challenge facing Basque of competing with sources of data and information from at least three hegemonic languages, namely Spanish, English and French (for different domains), it remains a daunting prospect to initiate and to justify Basque-only, separate and equal official documentation and information, especially in the critical fields of health-care delivery, medicine and drugs, social welfare, child protection and age-related advice. Critics make reference to a further sociolinguistic consideration, which is that many Basque speakers cannot communicate in Basque to other household members within a mixed language family or household context. This, detractors argue, further limits the strategy of applying Basque-only rules to citizens, even when they have registered to receive such services through Basque, because there may be valid circumstances when other members of the household would need to be able to share important information, such as reading medical guidance in the care of the very young or old, or details related to social security or tax matters. My own view is that if such considerations always hold sway then the logic of such a position is that lesser-used language speakers within bilingual societies will never be able to insist on their own language choice and hence this undermines the whole legal basis of the co-equality of languages—in fact as well as in law.

There has also been a systematic failure to gather and use the appropriate information, for if the administration is to respond to the citizens in the language of their choice, then it must have a permanent recorded knowledge of that choice. The fact is that the Basque Government has, over the past 30 years or so, created virtually no instruments to ensure that knowledge. Indeed, the bilingual-reply system mentioned above means that public servants did not have to pay attention to that choice. And even if one official knows what the choice of a particular citizen is today, that is no guarantee that s/he will know next week, nor that any other official will know. The solution to this problem seems—to informed insiders—to lie in the creation of a language-choice register, whereby citizens can register their language choice and, if computerized, the Basque Government computer-produced letters and communications could then be supplied in monolingual format according to that choice.[16]

In recent years the degree to which information technology and geographical information systems (GIS) has infused Basque officialdom has increased enormously and, in consequence, there has been a transition to a more informed public service choice element. The Basque Government has added to its stock of quantitative and qualitative procedures, and systematic statistical analysis and results, a series of follow-up thematic studies that throw light on subjects, such as attitudes towards language, immigrant opinions, inter-generational transmission, and so on. These are a very useful addition as they offer more detailed and nuanced interpretations of specific phenomena which are often overlooked in the more aggregate, multivariate analysis which the Basque system had pioneered in Europe.

The Basque Autonomous Community government has developed additional and different mechanisms, legal procedures, economical assignations, its own systematic research together with commissioning independent academic investigations to monitor and track processes and the results of its policies. The government is particularly strong on drawing on GIS analysis and interpretation from within its own ranks or those of the university sector or the Royal Basque Academy, which has an excellent GIS and interpretative capacity to track Basque and Spanish sociolinguistic change.

Thus, the implementation problem in no way seems to be related to lack of resources or ingenuity for there are substantial sums available for civil servant language training and there are a fair number of full-time planners, translators while other technical assistance is provided in the form of online dictionaries, terminology bank, spellchecker, and a wide range of computer programmes in Basque. It appears that there has simply been insufficient attention paid to evaluation and to outputs in terms of the need to deliver what government rhetoric claims is the citizen's rightful expectation—the delivery of government services in the language of one's choice. This is even more surprising as the Basque government has a very well-earned reputation for promoting Basque immersion, bilingual education and adult teaching across the statutory and non-statutory sectors.[17] Had such commitment been applied within public administration in a consistent manner then the legal basis for exercising language choice would have been matched by the active offer of government service; thus strengthening the perception and reality that successive Basque governments really are committed to the development of a fully functional bilingual society.

Is Irish Legislative Review a Short-hand for Policy Reduction?

If failure to implement standing legislation is one structural impediment to full bilingualism and the exercise of citizen choice and rights, then vacillating or reducing government commitment to safeguarding, promoting and regulating an official language is another tendency. For almost a century the Irish state has struggled with identifying what precisely its relationship is to Irish, both as a symbolic and as a communicative expression of its national identity. The struggle continues for a trio of worrying trends threaten to undermine the constitutionally guaranteed place of Irish in contemporary society and might even slow the process of reversing language shift which has been the hallmark of official language policy over recent decades. The 2012 government review of the operation and reach of the Irish Language Act 2003, together with proposed changes to the place of the Irish Language Commissioner within the system, when coupled with the financial retrenchment which has hit Irish-medium organizations particularly hard, all presage a reduced role for Irish in public life and limit the state's exposure to the protection and maintenance of the language despite formal constitutional guarantees.

Language-related legislation has characterized the Irish socio-legal system since the foundation of Saorstát Eireann in 1922. Then the Irish language acquired an official status under the Constitution Act of 1922. The revised Constitution of Ireland 1937 recognizes the Irish language as the native language of Ireland and the first official language. The English language is recognized as another official language. Article 8 of the Constitution set out the status of the Irish and English languages as follows:

> Article 8.1 The Irish language as the national language is the first official language
> Article 8.2 The English language is recognised as a second official language
> Article 8.3 Provision may, however, be made by law for the exclusive use of either of the said languages for any one or more official purposes, either throughout the State or in any part thereof.

These provisions have been the recourse of many citizens seeking redress to language rights issues over the years and, as a result, there is a considerable amount of case law concerning language issues. The necessity for citizens to seek redress to language rights in the Supreme Court has led to demands from NGOs and activists to mainstream considerations of language provisions when primary legislation was being drafted and consequently there are clauses to support the language in *c*. 160 specific provisions in Irish primary legislation. Notwithstanding these provisions, there was a perceived gap between the status afforded the language in the Constitution compared with the *de facto* rights afforded by the state to its Irish-speaking citizens. The social and educational infrastructure in support of Irish had been profoundly weakened by a series of policy reforms, chief of which was the decision taken in 1974 to end the system of compulsory Irish as a requirement for entry into the civil service. This had a knock-on effect on the ability of the state to deal with the public through Irish. It also heralded a trend by which court cases were launched in order to obtain services through Irish. Thus, the role of Irish as a statutory and service-delivery language was beginning to wane and a long-term campaign to restore the integral status and function of Irish culminated in the enactment of the Official Languages Act 2003.[18]

The 2003 Act is organized under five main parts:

> Part 1 Sections 1–4 Introduction and Definitions;
> Part 2 Sections 5–8 Houses of the Oireachtas (Parliament); Acts of the Oireachtas, the Courts;
> Part 3 Sections 11–18 Language Schemes;
> Part 4 Sections 20–30 the Language Commissioner; and Second Schedule
> Part 5 Sections 31–35 Place names.

The 2003 Act greatly enhanced the legal position of the language, building on constitutional case law and provisions in other major pieces of legislation, e.g. the Education Act of 1998 and Planning and Development Act 2000. The Act grants some fundamental rights to Irish language speakers. It ensures the right to use Irish in the Oireachtas (Houses of Parliament) and in all its committees. Simultaneous publication in Irish and English of all Acts of Parliament is also secured. The right to use Irish in any court is confirmed and the state must use the language chosen by the other party in civil cases. All witnesses are free to give evidence in their language of choice and the state shall not subject any citizen to any extra cost as a result of language choice. Simultaneous or consecutive translation shall be provided by the Court (Williams and Ó Flatharta, 2012).

The Act imposes a number of direct obligations on all public bodies. The citizen has the right to receive a reply in the original language of correspondence, be it

Irish or English, including electronic correspondence. Specified defined key documents shall be published simultaneously in Irish and English, e.g. annual reports and accounts, including certain strategic documents. Signage, stationery, mail shots and recorded public announcements shall be in Irish or in Irish or English.

The Act's principal mechanism for the delivery of bilingual services is its system of agreed language schemes, as adapted from the Welsh model formulated under the Welsh Language Act 1993 which obliged public bodies to treat both English and Welsh on the basis of equality and obliged named public bodies to implement language schemes (Williams, 2010). The Irish Minister responsible for language affairs may require any of the *c.* 650 public bodies to prepare and agree a language scheme which will detail the range of service in Irish in relation to official forms, information booklets, publications etc. The scheme establishes an element of language choice at the first point of contact, in providing a service on the telephone, a one-to-one service, on relevant websites and interactive services and has a particular focus for the delivery of Irish-language services in An Ghaeltacht.

When the head of the public body agrees a scheme with the Minister, the document becomes a statutory language plan for that organization for a set period of three years or until a new scheme is agreed. Schemes must indicate the level of services provided through the medium of English, through the medium of Irish or in Irish and English. Schemes must show how the provision of services through Irish will be improved in the following three years or until a new scheme is agreed. Language schemes are negotiated between the head of the public body and Department of Arts Heritage and Gaeltacht Affairs (AHGA) officials with commitments given to the use of Irish in relation to the following: (i) forms, brochures and other publications; (ii) first point of contact–reception staff; (iii) service provision on the telephone; (iv) one-to-one service through front-line staff; (v) services and advice provided electronically as in websites and other electronic media; (vi) interactive services (vii) services in Gaeltacht areas. Language schemes, once agreed between department officials and the head of the organization, are legal contracts creating rights for the citizen and obligations for the organization. When a scheme is agreed and ratified by the Minister the scheme cannot be renegotiated and must remain in place for the lifespan of the scheme or until replaced by a new scheme. Schemes must show particular regard to the provision of services through Irish to Gaeltacht areas (Irish-speaking areas defined by law). Once the scheme is agreed and ratified it passes from the Department of AHGA to the Language Commissioner's Office who is charged with the responsibility to ensure that the scheme is fully implemented.

Oifig Choimisinéir na dTeangacha Oifigiúla [The Office of the Official Languages Commissioner] was established under Part 4 of the Official Languages Act and forms a key part in the implementation structures of the Act.[19] While negotiation and agreement of language schemes is the responsibility of the Department of AHGA, monitoring compliance and investigation of complaints is the responsibility of the Language Commissioner. Foras na Gaeilge, the cross-border body established under the Good Friday Agreement 1999, charged with the promotion of the language, has no formal role under the Act. This was an attempt to separate the functions of language rights and obligations from the role of language promotion. This also reduces the amount of possible tension there may be between the regulatory and promotional aspects of language policy and provides—at the very least—a clear line of division, of reporting and of accountability, a feature not so fully appreciated in several other language regimes (Williams and Ó Flatharta, 2012).

A key feature of the Irish system is the requirement that the Minister provides a written annual report to the Houses of Parliament specifying to what extent and how in detail the Act has been implemented. When allied with the annual report of the Language Commissioner this provides a powerful tool for the analysis of the formal health and vitality of Irish as a public good.[20]

The Language Commissioner acts as a Compliance Agency, an Ombudsman Service and an Advisor on rights and obligations (Williams and Ó Flatharta, 2012). The Commissioner has a duty to monitor and ensure compliance by public bodies with the provisions of the Act. Complaints are received by email, telephone or by post and these are frequently resolved by advising the complainant. Between 2004 and 2009 the Commissioner's Office handled *c.* 3000 complaints from members of the public.[21] Many of these complaints arise from misunderstandings of what is and is not covered by the legislation in the Act. Between 2005 and 2010, 256 reviews and audits had been completed by the Language Commissioner. In some cases the complaint requires investigation, but most are resolved by reaching an agreement without having to go down the formal investigation route.

However, where such an agreement cannot be reached the Commissioner can move to a formal investigation.[22] In 2007, 10 such investigations were carried out; 17 were completed in 2008, 19 in 2009 and 11 in 2010. These investigations concern language rights and obligations which are held by the most significant bodies in the Irish public service, including ironically enough investigating issues of non-compliance in the Language Scheme of the Department of the Minister for Community, Equality and Gaeltacht Affairs. Consequently the independence of the office is of great importance when carrying out investigations and when seeking to press for remedial action in relation to the findings from the investigations which are presented in summary form in the annual report of the Commissioner. In order to guarantee against overt political interference or manipulation of the conduct of the office and course of investigations, or undue pressure on matters such as the level of staffing and resourcing, or spheres of competence, the Office of the Language Commissioner (OLC) has a statutory guarantee of independence under the Act.[23]

Independent research carried out since 2005 suggests that there are four main reasons for non-compliance and hence the need for intervention.[24] The first is the lack of an institution's capacity and resources to deliver services. The second is the lack of buy-in from senior management. The third is the internal communication of commitments is often lacking or not sufficiently explicit with few guidelines and deadlines set. The fourth is poor monitoring and review processes regarding the implementation and updating of the language schemes (Williams, 2009).

The Irish model has five principal strengths—the independence of the Commissioner, the separation of duties between promotion and regulation of language rights and policy, the monitoring function of the Office, the multi-year review and audit function and the option to investigate in cases of non-compliance. Of these the most vital is the system's guarantee of the independence of the office holder from influence or perceived influence from government, ministers, state departments, language organizations or other stakeholders. The Commissioner's independence is underpinned by provision in the Act whereby s/he may be removed from office only in the gravest of defined circumstances and only by the President of Ireland.

As an interim conclusion it may be stated that the Office has been established successfully and has secured the goodwill and support of the Irish language community. The Office fulfils its statutory duties with diligence and has confronted some difficult issues and has demonstrated its independence. However, even statutory independence is not guaranteed, for the government announced on 17 November 2011 that it had decided to merge the Oifig an Choimisinéara Teanga and transfer its functions to the Office of the Ombudsman. This has been interpreted as a serious threat to the language regime which has been so assiduously built up during this past decade. In the light of this proposal one may question what value might one place on Language Acts and the state's declared language policy and strategies? The Commissioner's role has been guaranteed by statutory edict, namely the Official Languages Act of 2003. What value and public confidence can one have in legally guaranteed independent agencies if they can be moved, shut and silenced without a great deal of public discussion and, more pertinently, overwhelmingly convincing logical arguments regarding their past performance?

It must be doubtful that there is any evidence whatsoever that the Commissioner's Office has been failing in its duties under its statutory obligations. In fact, it is generally understood that the Commissioner's Office has been very successful in both educating Irish citizens *vis-à-vis* their rights and in conducting investigations into non-compliance. A logical reading of the current decision might conclude that the principal reason why the Office has been threatened with abolition is that it has been too successful in highlighting the deficiencies in the Irish system and, as a consequence, the government has taken the decision to remove from the scene an agency which guarantees some degree of democratic accountability and redress for the inconsistent application of Irish language legislation. If this is so then such moves threaten the whole integrity of the state's commitment to the honouring of Irish as the first official language.

A second illustration is the review of the Official Languages Act 2003 carried out between winter 2011 and early summer 2012. In the briefing note announcing the review process it is stated that the Programme for Government contains the following commitment: "We will review the Official Languages Act to ensure expenditure on the language is best targeted towards the development of the language and that obligations are imposed appropriately in response to demand from citizens".

The objectives of the review are

> to ensure that the Act is an effective mechanism to support the development of the Irish language in an efficient and cost-effective manner and that the obligations arising from the Act are appropriate to ensure the satisfactory provision of services in Irish by public bodies, in line with public demand. (Government of Ireland, 2011)

Given this, the terms of reference have been framed with regard to the constitutional position of the Irish language, all existing legislation, the policy objectives of the

20-Year Strategy for the Irish language 2010–2030, and the relevant commitment in the Programme for Government.[25]

It is interesting to note that the tone of the review briefing note reflects current concern with cost-effectiveness, demand and rational behaviour. Nowhere does the review remit argue for a more robust system or the full implementation of the *20-Year Strategy* as a priority. Neither does it give an unequivocal guarantee that as a result of the review the position of Irish will not be weakened.

Other features combine to cause concern for Irish language supporters. The most immediate is the continued lack of implementation of the language schemes. In the past four years the number of schemes being submitted and/or approved has dwindled to nothing, this despite the fact that such trends occurred during the tenure of the champion of the Official Languages Act (OLA) process, Minister Éamon Ó Cuiv, and thus this failing cannot be laid at the door of the current government. It is very evident, both in terms of the weaknesses of the language scheme implementation process and in terms of the very low number of public servants charged with oversight of the OLA and language schemes, that the Irish language regime is not fully committed to the full realization of the OLA itself.

A longer-term difficulty is the regular threat made by Fine Gael, both while in opposition and now in government, that it is minded to change the status of Irish within the statutory education system from a core subject of the Leaving Certificate to an option within the curriculum to "better reflect the real demand for Irish in society". This is justified in terms of a lack of a popular demand for such skills in the workplace and reflects a broader neo-liberal discourse which seeks to make the Irish language less dependent on government subsidy, thereby forcing Irish speakers to bear the responsibility for the cost of maintaining a more vibrant set of networks and socio-cultural infrastructure. This is best illustrated by the manner in which the relationship between Foras na Gaeilge and its 19 core-funded organizations is being changed by the implementation of a New Funding Mode in 2012. Foras na Gaeilge were requested to review the sector, and propose recommendations of ways to rearrange it. Rather than consulting with the sector to assess the work currently being undertaken, or investigating new work methods for the sector, Foras na Gaeilge decided to put an end to funding for the 19 organizations who come under their auspices. It is evident that these organizations will not be able to function without core funding. To carry out work in the area of Irish language development and promotion, Foras na Gaeilge now plan to seek tenders for a limited number of projects which will last for only three years. The justification is that in leaner financial times only the essential and more innovative programmes will be funded. The cessation of their funding is a great cause for concern to the 19 core-funded organizations who believe that a competitive schemes approach will have a detrimental and irreversible effect on the Irish language in the years ahead. It is recognized that there is a need to develop and rearrange the sector in order to achieve both the best results, and value for money; however, the 2012 public consultation process on the New Funding Model was pre-empted by action taken by Foras na Gaeilge which disallows any opportunity given within the consultation document to express an opinion other than one which supports a new competitive funding model, of eight schemes, administered over a three-year period.[26]

It is doubtful if the review of the 2006 Act will tackle the three structural weaknesses identified by Williams and Ó Flatharta (2011). These are that the power to initiate language schemes rests with the political system, as the 'driver' of change is the Minister and department. The second is the Language Commissioner's lack of power to impose hard-hitting sanctions on public bodies for non-compliance. The third is that the Commissioner's staffing and finances is dependent on the political system, and thus the future of the Commissioner's independence, in political terms, is dependent on the government rather than guaranteed by law. Thus, while the framework of the constitution, the legal system and the general rhetoric of public policy all appear to be supportive of Irish language policy, the actual implementation and political culture appear lukewarm at best and antagonistic at worse. This leaves contemporary language strategists faced with seeking answers to a range of uncomfortable questions.

- What effect will the current review have on the future autonomy of the Language Commissioner?
- What effect will the continued reduction of public money have on the capacity of the Irish-speaking culture to flourish?
- What impact will these reforms have on the full implementation of the *20-Year Irish Language Strategy*?
- What effect will the downgrading of the constitutionally guaranteed national language have on the capacity of the system to deliver bilingual services, to operate in Irish, to engage with citizens in the language of their choice?
- What effect will there be on the psychology of the nation or on the vitality of Irish in the twenty-first century?

These are difficult questions indeed for any marginalized language group, made doubly difficult when they appear to be the product of a system which, at best, appears neutral toward the fortunes of the language and, at worst, downright hostile. The four challenges currently facing the Irish language within the formal apparatus of the state would appear to herald a new, and not so promising, dawn. The threat to the future of Irish within the education system relates to skills transmission and language reproduction. The review of the Official Languages Act 2003 is seen as signalling a downgrading of the state's commitment and exposure to the implications of formal legislation. The threat to merge the Language Commissioner's Office is interpreted as an attempt to reduce the impact of a vigorous champion of the language, while the New Funding Model is seen as a thinly veiled mechanism for committing less public money to civil society, many of whose partner organizations deliver vital bilingual services, in addition to the routine leisure, cultural and sports activities. It may be that as a result of civil society mobilization and robust opposition to many of these proposed changes that the medium-term future for Irish may not be as daunting as this quartet of socio-legal reforms suggest. There may yet arise small dots of light against the darkening gloom, but the source of such light appears to emanate from within civil society rather than the government and civil service.

The Expected Right is the Right to Expect

A third brief illustration of perfidious hope is the treatment of language rights in the current Welsh legislative model. Much of the justification for the replacement of the Welsh Language Act 1993 and its associated Welsh Language Board by a new Language Measure and its associated Language Commissioner by April 2012 was the introduction of a suite of language rights which could underpin the Welsh government's commitment to securing a bilingual society. Official discussion surrounding the Welsh Language (Wales) Measure 2011 (NAfW, 2011) was replete with references to the establishment of a new language regime within which citizens could exercise a choice in terms of their basic language rights in accordance with the promises made in the Cymru Un/One Wales concordat signed on 27 June 2007. However, the resultant Measure redefined the character of rights involved and trumpeted the "creation of a Welsh Language Commissioner with strong enforcement powers to protect the rights of Welsh speakers to access services through the medium of Welsh".

The Measure gives a prominent role to the Commissioner to be more than an Ombudsman, for the office holder is expected to be 'a champion for the Welsh language'. The language service standards derive from the full authority of the National Assembly for Wales and are thus meant to be read across all aspects of policy as part of the cross-cutting mandate of the Assembly's commitment to official bilingualism. The Commissioner has a strong regulatory function, but has also been allocated the responsibility of developing language rights in response to the implementation of new service standards. The Measure includes a Welsh Language Tribunal facility which is intended to scrutinize whether or not the Commissioner's investigations adhere to the letter of the law and thus forestall any 'rush' to test or challenge the Measure's application through the courts. Initially then the rights involved are the right to expect a service, rather than absolute rights as individuals in the field of education, health care, public administration and the like. That development is left for a later period of consolidation once the Commissioner's Office has secured the new system.

However, even now questions could also be raised as to how well-defined, clear, applicable and capable of development are language rights within the current model? One certain element likely to be of great concern, given the professionalization of the Canadian language policy process, is the need to be vigilant in finessing the relationship between systemic duties, individual rights and community vitality. Having pressed for a greater clarity with respect to individual language rights, it is very probable that Wales will face the Canadian issue of how to incorporate the needs of the community into language legislation. Doubtless, when the revised Welsh system is fully operational there will be some challenges.[27] Thus, consideration needs to be given now as to whether or not there are missing pieces of the jigsaw as, for example, a Welsh version of the Canadian Court Challenges/Language Rights Support Program (LRSP) (Foucher, 2010). In addition legislative devolution will surely be a major spur to the development of a more distinct Welsh legal profession and court system whose interpretation of public law will need to be evaluated and monitored.

Finally what does this legislative reform and construction of a new regulatory system mean in relation to the underlying rationale for the greater specification of the role of law in language protection? In Canada and Ireland the role of the Language

Commissioner is to protect, finesse and articulate the recognized language rights OCOL (2011). In Wales no such firm rights have been incorporated within legislation, except the 'right' to expect an equitable standard of service by nominated bodies. In that sense the Welsh model would appear to be an incomplete or immature version of an emerging international norm. However, that observation has to be tempered by reference to the fledgling emergence of legislative devolution and the slow evolution of a Welsh legal regime as it seeks to handle the increased demands of administrative law and a distinct Welsh interpretation of UK public life.

Conclusion

Clearly much of the routine implementation of language legislation has not fallen foul of the deleterious tendencies I have highlighted here—yet! Fiscal pressures, the hollowing out of the state, the over-professionalization of language policy and planning as a handmaiden to state regulation and the atrophying role of a robust civil society in the promulgation of language affairs, all suggest that without due vigilance many of the gains made in the past two generations could simply be reversed either by benign neglect or by wilful damage.

The delivery of linguistically differentiated public services is a major area of public policy and has ramifications at all levels in the political hierarchy from the EU down to the level of the local council. Consequently future research in this field could usefully be directed towards tracing the impact of EU legislation on language rights,[28] on how the constitutional order which the EU represents might play in relation to the harmonization of official, but not state-wide, languages, such as Basque, Catalan and Welsh. Within the UK, consideration should be given to the manner in which the Equality and Human Rights Commission and the Single Equality Act might run to extending discrimination law to include language and individual citizen rights. There might also be a need for firm, time-series evidence and analysis to trace the contours of community vitality, as, following the Canadian precedent, there may yet be a new emphasis on the necessity of specifying and securing community language rights within public law. Perfidious hope may yet give way to public gain in matters of language legislation, but only if the respective minority language is treated as a public good and not seen as an outmoded expression of historical special pleading.

Acknowledgements

This work was facilitated by a grant from the British Academy, 'Official Language Commissioners' (SG 50880) and an ESRC grant 'The Office of Language Commissioner in Wales, Ireland and Canada' (Ref ES/J003093/1) which are gratefully acknowledged. I am grateful to an anonymous referee and Prof. A. Cole, Cardiff University for their advice.

Notes

[1]A case in point is POBAL's (2006) draft Bill for an Irish Language Act in Northern Ireland, which was revised in 2012.

[2]The case was *D and H* v. *Czech Republic* (2008) 47 EHRR 3, cited in Ahmed (2011: 30).

[3]As one of the chief components of group identity and the means by which the ideas and techniques of social development are diffused, language has become one of the most sensitive issues of the contemporary world. Mackey (1991: 51) estimated that there were some 6170 living languages exclusive of dialects. This rich inheritance has to be contained and managed within 195 or so sovereign states and, if we admit dependencies and semi-autonomous polities, the number rises to over 200. Consequently, there is a lack of congruence between the international political system and the cultural inheritance of its constituent citizens. This suggests that there will be a near-permanent crisis involving attempts to maintain linguistic diversity in the face of increasing linguistic standardization in many parts of the world.

[4]At the same time the USA passed two Native American Languages Acts designed to promote the freedom of Native Americans to speak and develop their mother tongue. The Law on Languages of the Russian Federation enacted in 1991 conferred the status of a national property on all languages and placed them under the protection of the state. In 1991, the Colombian Constitution gave autochthonous languages official status in their own territories. UNESCO and the UN have also produced statements in support of linguistic and cultural diversity. Nic Craith (2007: 180) argues that such developments have enhanced the status of languages world-wide and generated a new interest in the concept of linguistic human rights.

[5]Interview wtih Miren Azkarate (former Minister of Culture, Basque Government, 2000–08), Bilbao, 12 Oct 2011.

[6]Aitzel's main aim was to promote and enrich the Basque language in a progressive manner for he was deeply involved with the Modernists and with writers such as Garcia Lorca. He adopted a largely pragmatic approach, shunning much of the conventional ideological doctrine. I was delighted to deliver the plenary address at the joint Basque Academy and UPV conference held in his honour in Bilbao on 14 Oct 2011.

[7]A National Conference of the Congress had contacted individuals in Wales, Belgium, Switzerland, Canada and Luxembourg to ascertain what kind of bilingual education guidance could be adopted as best practice policies.

[8]Information as given at interview by Miren Azkarate, Bilbao, 12 Oct 2011.

[9]In the later period the activists did not follow this model, although Gipuzkoa did publish the writings of Aitzel, but hardly anyone had paid attention to him in the contemporary period until 2011 when an attempt was made to 'revindicate' his name.

[10]Please see Hikuntza Politikarako Sailburuordetza (2008: 55) for the 14 programme themes.

[11]Gardner *et al.* (2000: 326) report that the insistence by some nationalists to strengthen the differentiation between 'them' and 'us' (i.e. between Basque and Spanish) has had consequences in corpus planning, as it has led purism in vocabulary, neologism being coined on the basis of really or supposedly authentic Basque roots avoiding any Romance input. This purism, though satisfying for the élite proposing it, has not facilitated the spread of new vocabulary and has possibly alienated some users.

[12]The Basque Government has frequently been a coalition, but until 2009 the dominant party has nearly always been nationalist, as reflected in the fact that the government's *lehendakari* or president has always been a nationalist.

[13]For statistics, please visit the Basque Government website (www.euskara.euskadi.net) and select the EAS statistics bank: the text is also available in English.

[14]It leaves asides specific schemes for education, health sector, police and the administration of justice.

[15]A more positive finding is the numbers of permanent post holders in posts without dates of compulsion yet having a certified achievement of the required level and in the numbers of temporary post holders in posts of both types with certified achievement.

[16]These failings were identified to me at successive interviews and by correspondence with senior civil servants and government Ministers, past and present. Of course, a counter-argument could be put, that given that so many of the bilingual citizens would probably opt for a Spanish form, then providing a bilingual version automatically at least provides the possibility that some might opt to return their correspondence in Basque.

[17]For a prescient overview of Basque education, see Gardner and Zalbide (2005).

[18]The Official Languages Act is considered to be influenced by international experience, mainly the Official Languages Acts of Canada of 1969 and 1988, and the Welsh Language Act, 1993.

[19]The Language Commissioner is appointed by the President of Ireland on the advice of government and the approval of the Houses of the Parliament. Mr Seán Ó Cuirreáin was appointed as the first Language Commissioner by the President on 24 Feb 2004 for a six-year period as set out in the legislation. The Commissioner was reappointed for a second six-year term on the 23 Feb 2010 after receiving full support from all political parties in the Parliament.

[20]In addition to the reporting duties attached to conducting investigations the Commissioner is required by legislation to provide an annual report, in each of the official languages, of the activities of his office for that year to the Minister for AHGA to be laid before the Houses of the Oireachtas.

[21]The office is in An Spidéal in the Galway Gaeltacht. The office is financed from public finances through the Department of AHGA and, in 2009, received a budget of €796 000.

[22]The Commissioner's Annual Reports since 2007 provide detail on investigations examining specific complaints from members of the public or investigating specific bodies that fail to implement initiatives agreed in their language scheme.

[23]This is a status which approaches that enjoyed by the Canadian Federal Commissioner of Official Languages, and is slightly different from the current provisions of the Welsh Language Commissioner (Williams, 2011).

[24]Similar issues arise in Finland, Wales and the Basque Country. See Sandberg *et al.* (2011) for details of the 'From Act to Action project' and, for Wales, see Williams (2010).

[25]The terms of reference for the review are published on the Department's website (www.ahg.gov.ie). The review was led by officials from the Department of AHGA, who consulted with key stakeholders, including the Office of An Coimisinéir Teanga, government departments, other public bodies, Irish language and Gaeltacht organizations, general public and international experts. On completion, the Minister will make recommendations to be considered by the full government.

[26]A bilingual consultation document containing 108 pages was issued by Foras na Gaeilge. The length and complexity of this document provides a challenge to the public in answering the questionnaire. While public meetings and focus groups were held, a process such as this normally focuses on written submissions, and detractors claim that the operative questionnaire was inaccessible to the public, in both languages. Further information about the New Funding Model is available online at http://www.gaelport.com/samhailnuamhaoinithe, and the consultation document can be accessed at www.gaeilge.ie/samhail.

[27]Legal experts have suggested to me that if the Scottish precedent holds true, there will be far less instances than expected as civil society tends to be 'tolerant' of the need for devolved powers to bed in and be given time to work and adapt to a new legal system.

[28]One such comprehensive account may be found in Ahmed (2011), see especially pp. 146–168.

References

Ahmed, T. (2011), *The Impact of EU Law on Minority Rights*. Oxford: Hart Publishing.

An Coimisinéir Teanga (2010), *Annual Report*. An Spidéal: An Coimisinéir Teanga. Available at http://www.coimisineir.ie/downloads/TuarascailBhliantuil2010.pdf (accessed 11 December 2012).

Breziger, B. (2010), From Maastricht to Lisbon. The Development of Language Legislation in EU Treaties, Paper presented at the International Conference of the International Academy of Linguistic Law "Language, Law and the Multilingual State", University of the Free State, 1–3 November, 2010.

Cairney, P. (2012), *Understanding Public Policy*. Basingstoke: Palgrave.

Dunbar, R. (2007), Diversity in addressing diversity; Canadian and British legislative approaches to linguistic minorities and their international legal context, in C.H. Williams (ed.), *Language and Governance*, pp.104–58. Cardiff: University of Wales Press.

Foucher, P. (2010), Language Rights and the Canadian Jurisprudence. Paper presented at the International Conference of the International Academy of Linguistic Law "Language, Law and the Multilingual State", University of the Free State, 1–3 November, 2010.

Gardner, N., Puigdevall i Serralvo, M. and Williams, C. H. (2000), Language Revitalization in Comparative Context: Ireland, the Basque Country and Catalonia, in C.H. Williams (ed.), *Language Revitalization*, pp.311–361. Cardiff: University of Wales Press.

Gardner, N. and Zalbide, M. (2005), Basque Acquisition Planning, *International Journal of the Sociology of Language*, Vol.174, pp.55–72.

Government of Ireland (2003), *The Official Languages Act*. Dublin: Government of Ireland. Available at http://www.irishstatutebook.ie/2003/en/act/pub/0032/index.html (accessed 11 December 2012).

Government of Ireland (2011) *Review of the Official Language Act 2003*. Dublin: Department of Arts, Heritage and the Gaeltacht.

Hikuntza, Politikarako Sailburuordetza (2008), *2005–2009 Legealdiko Jarduera-Txostena*. Gasteiz: Eusko Jaurlaritzia.

Janis, M. W., Kay, R. S. and Bradley, A. W. (2008), *European Human Rights Law*. Oxford: Oxford University Press.

Mackey, W.F. (1991), Language Diversity, Language Policy and the Sovereign State, *History of European Ideas*, Vol.13, pp.51–61.

National Assembly for Wales (2011), *Welsh Language (Wales) Measure 2011*. Cardiff: National Assembly for Wales.

Nic Craith, M. (2007), Rethinking Language Policies: Challenges and Opportunities, in C.H. Williams (ed.), *Language and Governance*, pp.159–87. Cardiff: University of Wales Press.

OCOL (2011), *Annual Report 2009–2010*. Ottawa: OCOL.

POBAL (2006), *Proposals for an Irish Language Act for Northern Ireland*. Belfast: POBAL.

Sandberg, O' Flatharta and Williams (2011), *From Act to Action*, Report Submitted to the Svensak Kulturfonden, Helsinki.

Viceconsejeria de Politica Linguistica (2008), *Memoria de la Legislature 2005–2009*. Vitoria: Gobierno Vasco.

Williams, C. H. (2009), Foras na Gaeilge and Bwrdd yr Iaith Gymraeg: Yoked But Not Yet Shackled, *Irish Studies Review*, Vol.17, No.1, pp.55–88.

Williams, C. H. (2010), From Act to Action in Wales, in D. Morris (ed.), *Welsh in the Twenty-First Century*, pp.36–60. Cardiff: University of Wales Press.

Williams, C. H. and Ó Flatharta, P. (2012), *The Office of the Language Commissioner, Ireland. The Impact of the Commission on Irish Language Policy and Official Strategy*. Bloemfontein: University of the Free State.

Woeherling, J. (2010), The Supreme Court of Canada and the Object, Nature and Foundations of Linguistic Rights, in Programme for the 12th International Conference of the International Academy of Linguistic Law "Language, Law and the Multilingual State", University of the Free State, 1–3 November, 2010 (Abstract), p.115.

Index

Academic Councils for Regional Languages 31
accountability 109, 115
adherent language policy 68, 72–3
agenda-setting 23, 102
Ahmed, T. 103
Aitzel 105–6
Aléria affair 33
Algeria 33
Alsace 4
Alsatian language 40
ancien regime 29
Anglesey County Council (ACC) 72–3
anti-Semitism 29
Arabic language 1
area studies 3
Association of Individuals of Silesian Nationality (SONŚ) 53, 56
asymmetrical endogenous institutionalization 28, 43
Austrian Empire 50
autonomy 7, 11, 23, 34–5, 47; legislation 105, 117; linguistic rights 96; party systems 53; Upper Silesia 50–3, 56, 60, 62

Baltic States 104
barriers to entry 15
Basque Country 1–2, 5, 8, 53, 67–76, 88, 93, 104–11
Basque language 31, 40, 104–11, 119
Basque Promotion Directorate 78
Belgium 5, 28, 40, 42–3
bilingualism 31, 33, 37–8, 40, 70–1; comparison 73, 75, 81; legislation 102, 104–5, 107–11, 117–18
Bizkaia Provincial Council (BPC) 72–3, 75–8
blocked articulation mechanisms 7, 16–22, 24
Bohemia 49
Boon, D. 42
Breton language 2, 29, 31–2, 36–41
Breton Language Office 38–9
Breziger, B. 104
British Isles 37
Brittany 4, 31, 33, 36–40, 42–4
Brittany Cultural Charter 39
Brittany Cultural Council (CCB) 39
Brittany Cultural Institute (ICB) 39
Brittany Regional Council 38
Broudic, F. 37
Brubaker, R. 49, 62
bureaucracy 75, 108

Cairney, P. 102–3
Canada 5, 28, 109, 118–19
capitalism 9–10, 29
Carlin, P. 5, 67–85
case studies 29, 68, 73–5
Castilian language 8–9, 11–16, 18–19, 23
Catalan language 9, 11–13, 15–16, 18–19, 24; comparison 70–1, 73–4; legislation 104, 119; role 31, 40
Catalonia 1, 3–5, 8–10, 13–26, 38–40; language policy 10–13, 67–76; legislation 104–5; linguistic rights 88, 93; nationalism 7–26
Catholicism 29, 37, 40, 50, 58
Celtic languages 37
Central Europe 47
centralization 29–32
centre-periphery relations 3–4, 68, 76
Centro de Investigaciones Sociológicas (CIS) 16, 18
Cerquiglini, B. 42

Charter for Regional and Minority Languages 3, 30, 56, 104
Chinese language 1
Christianity 54, 79
Ch'ti 41
citizenship 102, 104
civil service 4–5, 32, 76, 102, 108–9, 111, 117
Civil Service Laws 72
civil society 4, 36–40, 102, 117, 119
class 8–10, 12–16, 18, 23, 68, 78, 107
clientelism 34
Cole, A. 1–6, 27–46
collective entities 94–6
Commission for Racial Equality 71
communism 47, 50, 57, 59, 70
communitarianism 5, 28
conscription 29
Constitution Act 111
Constitutional Council 36, 40
Consultative Agency on the Basque Language 106
Convention against Discrimination at School 2–3, 30
corporate entities 92–6
La Corse 34
Corse Matin 34
Corsica 4, 41–3
Corsican Assembly 34–5
Corsican language 29, 31–6, 40–1
Corsican Regionalist Action 33
Council of Europe 3, 30, 104
Craith, N. 104
Creole languages 40, 55
Czech language 50
Czech Republic 103
Czechoslovakia 49–50

Dahl, R. 14
Darwin, C. 87
Days of the Upper Silesian Heritage 55
Deixonne Law 31–2, 41–2
Dembinska, M. 3–4, 47–66
democracy 7–11, 13–16, 23, 68, 70; comparison 79–80, 83; legislation 102, 106, 115; linguistic rights 87–8; Spain 74
demographics 7, 9–12, 16, 37, 53, 75
demolinguistics 74, 76–8, 104
Department of Arts Heritage and Gaeltacht Affairs (AHGA) 113
Deutsch, K. 2
devolution 28, 33–4, 71, 81, 118–19
dialects 3, 29–30, 32, 37, 41–2; legislation 105; Upper Silesia 48, 51, 54–6, 59
dictionaries 55, 111
diglossia 33, 41
divided society 8–10
Diwan association 37–8, 40
Dolińska, K. 57, 60–1
Dunbar, R. 104
Dworkin, R. 90

East 54
Economic and Social Research Council (ESRC) 37
economics 10, 33, 36, 38, 57; legislation 105, 107; linguistic rights 88; Upper Silesia 62
education 11–13, 16, 18–19, 29, 32; Brittany 37–8, 40; Corsica 33, 35; France 31; legislation 101, 103, 105–7, 111–12, 116–18; linguistic rights 88; Picard language 41; Upper Silesia 58
Education Act 112
Education Code 31
electoral market failure 15
elites 4, 9, 15–16, 19, 23–4, 48–9, 81
employment 10, 13, 38, 40, 57–8, 105–11
English language 30, 59, 110–13
Equality and Human Rights Commission 119
erabilera-planak 107
ethnogenesis 54–6
ethnolects 48–9, 51, 54–5, 58–9
ethnolinguistic mobilizations 1–5; Catalonia 7–26; comparison 67–86; France 27–46; legislation 101–22; linguistic rights 87–99; Upper Silesia 47–66
Ethnolinguistic Mobilizations and Regional Languages in Europe 1
Eurasia 47
Euromosaic polls 36
Europe 1–5, 10, 27–8, 36, 49; legislation 101, 103–4, 106, 110; and Upper Silesia 53–5, 57, 61–3
European Consortium for Political Research 1
European Convention on Human Rights 103
European Court of Human Rights 53, 103
European Union (EU) 2, 47, 53, 57, 59, 103–4, 119

evaluation 103, 111

fascism 29
Feller-Carton method 41
Ferry Laws 29
Fifth Republic 39
Finland 104
First World War 29, 50, 55
fiscal capacities 75–6
Flanders 2
Foras na Gaeilge 113, 116
France 2, 4, 27–46
France 3 32, 34
France Bleue Frequenza Mora 34
Franco, F. 9–10, 24
free trade 9
French language 29–33, 35, 37, 40–2, 110
French Ministry of Culture 29, 42
French Ministry of National Education 31
French Revolution 29
future generations 88, 92, 94, 96–7

Gaelic language 104
Gajda, J. 51, 55
Galicia 8, 82
Gallo languages 37, 40–1
General Delegation for the French Language 29
geographical information systems (GIS) 110–11
German language 50, 58–9, 61
Germany 1, 49–50, 55, 60
Gipuzkoa Provincial Council (GPC) 72, 75–6
Girondins 44
Giscard d'Estaing, V. 39
globalization 58
González, F. 10
Good Friday Agreement 113
Gorzelik, J. 52–4
Gourvil, F. 37
governance 14, 67–8, 73, 77, 80, 82, 105
government legislation 102, 107–9, 111, 116–17
grammar 56
Great Britain *see* United Kingdom
Green, L. 91
group rights 92–6
groupness 48–9, 52–7, 62
Gwynedd County Council 69, 71–3, 75, 82

Haby Law 31
Hapsburgs 55
Harguindéguy, J.-B.P. 1–6, 27–46
Hebrew language 1
hegemony 4, 7–26, 29, 76–7, 101, 110
High Council of Languages and Cultures from France 42
historiography 48, 54, 62
Hroch, M. 48, 54, 57, 62–3
human rights 103
Human Rights Law 103
Humphreys, H.L. 37

identity 28, 36, 48–57, 59–63, 91; comparison 82–3; legislation 104, 107; linguistic rights 93; Upper Silesia 62
ideology 9, 12, 14, 16, 23–4; comparison 73, 76, 79; France 29, 44; legislation 105–6; Upper Silesia 57, 60
imagined communities 4, 54, 68
immersion 31, 33, 40, 111
implementation 102–3, 116
individual rights 90–2, 118
industrialism 9
institutional systems 76–82
international diffusion 28, 43
international law 103–4
Internet discussions 58
Interreg Programme 35
Ireland 2, 5, 105, 108–9, 111–18
Irish language 2, 104, 111–13, 115–17
Irish Language Act 111
Irish Language Commissioner 111
ISO codes 56
Italian language 32
Italy 3, 33, 35

Jacobin Republic 4, 27–46
Janicki, W. 48
Janis, M. 103
Jerczyński, D. 54–5
John Paul II, Pope 58, 61
Jones, P. 90, 92–3, 95
justice 28, 88–9, 102

Kamusella, T. 55–6, 59
Karasiewicz, L. 56
Kashubian language 56–7
Kijonka, T. 52
Kożdón, J. 51, 55
Kurcz, Z. 54, 57–8
Kymlicka, W. 88

Laffin, M. 80, 81

Lamaxeta 105
Lang, J. 40
language 1–5; Catalonia 7–26; centralization 29–32; comparison 67–86; France 27–46; legislation 101–22; policy 67–85; rights 87–100; Upper Silesia 47–66
Language Commissioner's Office 113–15, 117–19
Language Normalization Plans 72–3
Language Policy Law 79
Language Rights Support Program (LRSP) 118
Latin America 11
Latin language 29
Law for the Normalization of the use of Basque 107
leadership 109
legal rights 89
legislation development 74–5, 94, 101–22
legislative turn 101–22
legitimation 102
lengua propia 74–5
Lewis, H. 5, 87–99
lexis 56
liberalism 5, 13, 15, 28, 30, 79, 102
Library of Congress 56
Lincoln, A. 40
Linguistic Law 80
linguistic rights 87–99, 104–5, 107, 113–14, 118–19
Lizarra-Estella Agreement 77
Lizeadi 105
Louis Richard Theatre 42
loyalty conversion 60

Mahoney, J. 89
Manresa 72–3
Mansvelt Beck, J. 76
Marfany, J.L. 9
Mauroy, P. 35
Maurras, C. 29
media 4–5, 11, 33–4, 40, 53, 79, 88, 101–2
Mediterranean 32
Middle Ages 41
Miley, T.J. 4, 7–26
military 4, 29
Minorities Law 47, 55–6, 62
Mitterrand, F. 31
modernism 2, 87
Moore, C. 57
moral rights 89–95, 97
Movement for the Autonomy of Silesia (RAŚ) 52–3, 55–6, 60, 62
multiculturalism 28, 43, 61

nation-building 7–8, 11–13, 15, 23, 27; comparison 77, 79; France 41; Upper Silesia 47–66
National and Ethnic Minorities Law 54
nationalism 2–4, 7–26, 28, 33–5, 43–4, 76–80, 82, 105–7
Nazism 39
neo-elitism 23
neo-liberalism 75, 116
Niedźwiedzki, D. 60
Nijakowski, L.M. 52, 60
Nobel Prize 55
non-governmental organizations (NGOs) 104, 112
Normalization of the Use of Basque Law 72
North Africa 11

Ó Cuiv, É. 116
Ó Flatharta, P. 117
Occitan (Oc) language 2, 31, 40–1
Official Languages Act 112–17
Ofis ar Brezhonneg 38
Oïl languages 40–3
ontology 89, 91–4, 97
orthography 41, 56

Paoli, P. 32–3
participatory goods 92
party systems 1, 11–16, 18, 23–4, 74; Catalonia 70; comparisons 76–82; Corsica 34–5; Ireland 116; legislation 106–7; Picard 42; Upper Silesia 51–7, 62
patois 29, 41
Pétain, P. 29
Picard dialect 29, 32, 40–4
Picardy Regional Council 42
Planning and Development Act 112
Plura, M. 56
pluralism 2, 44, 102, 104
Poland 4, 47–56, 59, 62–3
policy-making 10–13, 16, 18–19, 28–33, 38, 67–85, 102–7
Polish language 50–1, 58–9
political science 1, 3–4, 28
political theory 3, 5, 28, 88–90, 93, 96
polyarchy 14
Ponte-Novu, battle of 32
Popieliński, P. 60–1

post-modernism 61
Potsdam Agreement 50
poverty 13
pre-emptive language policy 68–71
pressure groups 1, 40
principal-agent relations 15
Pro Loquela Silesiana 56
Protestantism 50
Prussia 50
psychology 91, 117
public goods 94–5, 119
public opinion 12, 14, 24, 39
public sector 11, 13, 108
Public Service Law 107
public sphere 30, 52–4, 59, 62
Pujol, J. 10–11

Quebec 88, 91

Radio France 32, 34
Radio France Outre-mer 32
Radio Golfe 34
Rawls, j. 28
Raz, J. 89, 94, 96
Réaume, D. 90–2
regional language role 1–5
regional studies 3, 28
Regional Training Plan 35, 36
reluctant language policy 68, 73–4
republicanism 9, 27–46
resistance 24
rhetoric 105–11, 117
rights 87–99, 101–5, 107, 109, 111, 113–14, 118–19
Roczniok, A. 56
Rokkan, S. 36
Roller, E. 80
Roma 103
Ross, C. 76, 80
Royal Basque Academy 105, 111
Rygjou, A. 55

Santa Coloma de Gramenet (SCG) 69–71, 75, 79, 82
Sardinia 32
Sarkozy, N. 34
Savary Decree 31
Schumpeter, J. 23
Second World War 29, 32, 39, 50
Secretariat for Language Policy 79
segregation 8
Sicilian language 3
signposting 38
Silesia 4, 47–66
Silesian Academic Association 53
Silesian language 47–63
Silesian League 51
Silesian National Publishing House 56
Single Equality Act 119
Slavic languages 54
Slovenia 104
social mobility 12–13, 24
social movements 1–3, 8, 28, 43–4
socialism 19, 24, 35, 38, 40; comparisons 73, 78, 80; legislation 106–7
socio-linguistics 3–4
sociology 3, 8, 56–8, 60, 93
soft law 77
Soviet Union 2, 50, 55
Spain 2, 5, 7–12, 15, 19; and Catalonia 24; comparisons 80; democracy 74; and France 28; legislation 106–7
Spanish Civil War 10, 106
Spanish language 70, 72–4, 106, 109–11
Sroka 55
state languages 1–4, 27–8, 71, 87
State-Region Plans 36
succession 103
survival rights 90–6
Swahili language 1
Swedish language 104
Świątkiewicz-Mosny, M. 58

Tambor, J. 55
taxation 75, 82, 102, 110
Taylor, C. 91
termination 103
Tes 38
Third Republic 29
Thomas, A. 81
Thompson, J. 96
Toubon Law 30
translation services 38, 42, 71, 111
triglossia 32

unemployment 10, 57–8
UNESCO 2, 29
Union of People of Silesian Nationality (ZLNS) 53
Union of Soviet Socialist Republics (USSR) *see* Soviet Union
unions 40, 71
United Kingdom (UK) 5, 71, 80, 119
United States (US) 5
University of Amiens 41
University of Corte 33
University of Picardie 41
University of Silesia 62

University of Villeneuve d'Ascq 41
Upper Silesia 47–66
Urla, J. 76
Urwin, D.W. 36

Van Dyke, V. 93
Van Morgan, S. 82
Veneto language 3
vernacular languages 1, 32, 48, 59
Versailles, Treaty of 32
Villers-Cotterêts Decree 32
Vives, V. 9
Voce Nustrale 34

Wales 2–3, 5, 38–40, 67–76, 118–19; legislation 105, 109; linguistic rights 88, 93
Walloon 41–2
Weber, M. 29
welfare state 14–15
Welsh Assembly 76, 81, 118
Welsh language 71, 73, 75, 80–1, 104; legislation 113, 118–19
Welsh Language Act (WLA) 71, 73, 75, 113, 118–19
Welsh Language Board 118
Welsh Language Commissioner 118
Welsh Language Measure 81, 118
Welsh Language Tribunal 118
Welsh Office 71
West 5, 28, 87
Wikipedia 56
Williams, C.H. 5, 101–22
Woeherling, J. 105
Woźniczka, Z. 62
Wróblewski, P. 54
Wyderka, B. 55

xenophobia 9–10

Yugoslavia 2